I0225639

PREACHING EPHESIANS

PROCLAMATION:
Preaching the New Testament

Before the rise of historical criticism as the dominant mode of interpretation in the eighteenth century, biblical commentaries were written for the church with homiletical interests in mind. Since the Enlightenment, the critical commentary has largely excluded ecclesiastical and homiletical interests. In introducing the Meyer series in 1831, H. A. W. Meyer set the standard for subsequent commentaries, indicating that this commentary would exclude philosophical and ecclesiastical concerns and would concentrate on what the original authors meant in their own historical context.

This standard creates a challenge for preachers whose task is to bring a living word to listeners, most of whom did not come to church out of antiquarian interests. Some commentaries have attempted to overcome the gap between the historical interests of the critical commentary and the homiletical concerns of the preacher by publishing parallel sections—one providing critical scholarship and the other offering guidance for preaching.

While biblical scholars specialize in a specific genre or book of Scripture, preachers are responsible for interpreting the entire canon over an extended time. As commentaries are increasingly complex, few preachers have the opportunity to mine the information and reflect an awareness of contemporary scholarship on each passage. Thus they face the challenge of merging the horizons between critical scholarship and a living word for the congregation. The living in the past, or to ignore exegesis for the sake of relevance.

In these volumes, scholar-preachers and preacher-scholars offer a guide for preachers, bringing the horizons of past and present together. The series is not a typical commentary, but a guide for preachers that offers the results of scholarship for the sake of preaching. Writers in this series will reflect an awareness of critical scholarship but will not focus on the details involved in a commentary. Rather, they will offer the fruits of critical scholarship reflected in explanations of section of the biblical text. After a brief discussion of the major issues in a book—the central issues—each volume will be arranged by sections with an eye to what is useful for the sermon.

Authors in the Proclamation series will describe the major focus of each section, recognizing the place of the passage in the context of the book. Authors will look to the rhetorical impact of the text, asking "what does the text do." Does it reassure the hearers? Does it lead them in worship and praise? Does it indict? Does it encourage? The Proclamation series will guide preachers in recognizing the essential rhetorical focus of the passage towards representing the impact of the text for today.

While preachers offer a living word for a specific situation, they also speak to larger cultural issues that face every congregation. Consequently, writers in this series may employ their knowledge of the ancient situation to suggest how the ancient word speaks across the centuries to parallel situations in our own time.

Accompanying the discussion writers may employ sermons, outlines, or other resources that further empower today's preachers in making the use of scholarship for the good of the church today.

Series Editors:

James W. Thompson is Scholar in Residence at the Graduate School of Theology as well as the editor for Restoration Quarterly.

Jason A. Myers is Associate Professor of Biblical Studies at Greensboro College, Greensboro, NC.

PREACHING EPHESIANS

Lynn H. Cohick

CASCADE *Books* • Eugene, Oregon

PREACHING EPHESIANS

Proclamation: Preaching the New Testament

Copyright © 2025 Lynn H. Cohick. All rights reserved. Except for brief quotations in critical publications or reviews, no part of this book may be reproduced in any manner without prior written permission from the publisher. Write: Permissions, Wipf and Stock Publishers, 199 W. 8th Ave., Suite 3, Eugene, OR 97401.

Cascade Books
An Imprint of Wipf and Stock Publishers
199 W. 8th Ave., Suite 3
Eugene, OR 97401

www.wipfandstock.com

PAPERBACK ISBN: 978-1-6667-0694-9
HARDCOVER ISBN: 978-1-6667-0695-6
EBOOK ISBN: 978-1-6667-0696-3

Cataloguing-in-Publication data:

Names: Cohick, Lynn H. [author].

Title: Preaching Ephesians / by Lynn H. Cohick.

Description: Eugene, OR: Cascade Books, 2025 | Series: Proclamation: Preaching the New Testament | Includes bibliographical references.

Identifiers: ISBN 978-1-6667-0694-9 (paperback) | ISBN 978-1-6667-0695-6 (hardcover) | ISBN 978-1-6667-0696-3 (ebook)

Subjects: LCSH: Bible.—Ephesians—Commentaries. | Bible.—Ephesians—Criticism, interpretation, etc. | Bible.—New Testament—Homiletical use.

Classification: BS2695.53 C645 2025 (print) | BS2695.53 (ebook)

Cohick, Lynn H. "Citizenship and Empire: Paul's Letter to the Philippians and Eric Liddell's Work in China." *JSPL* 1.2 (2011) 14–16. (https://doi.org/10.2307/26426484) Used with permission from Penn State University Press.

To Josiah Michael, Jonathan Andrew, and Elisabeth Dianna Cohick

May you know the love of Christ that surpasses knowledge

CONTENTS

ACKNOWLEDGEMENTS

I AM GRATEFUL TO James W. Thompson and Jason A. Myers for their invitation to participate in this timely commentary series focused on preparing preachers to offer the living word to their congregations. Their encouragement and feedback strengthened the manuscript. Michael Thomson, Acquisitions Editor at Wipf & Stock, showed me characteristic patience and cheerfulness as the project moved to completion. I am indebted to Scot McKnight for his close reading of the draft; any mistakes which remain are entirely my fault. I am especially grateful to Tara Beth Leach, friend and pastor who dialogued with me over several meals about preaching Ephesians; Tara Beth, I hope I captured your insight and wisdom throughout this commentary.

Many thanks to my husband, Jim, who read the page proofs, saying several times how much he liked the book. I hope readers will have a similar experience.

INTRODUCTION TO EPHESIANS

EPHESIANS TELLS THE STORY of God's redemption plan. Throughout the letter, the careful reader discerns the grand narrative that underpins Paul's message. As with all good stories, the plot is riveting. Ephesians highlights the creation of God's people adopted in Christ, tracing back through the promises of the Old Testament and forward from the present life of the church, Christ's body. The center of the story is Christ's redemptive work on the cross, which has two equally important results: the cross brought forgiveness of sins and created a new people unified in him. The drama happens not only at the human level, but engages with the cosmos, as spiritual forces, some of them antithetical to God's work, marvel at God's redemptive plan. The cosmic dimension of the story includes a time before creation when God in God's Self determined this redemptive plan to be executed by the three persons of the Trinity: Father, Son, and Holy Spirit. The plan looks forward to the culmination when all things will be united in Christ.

The characters in the drama are as compelling as the story itself. The Ephesians come from all walks of life and all ages, captivated by the promise of an inheritance based on adoption as God's beloved child. In a surprise twist, Jew and gentile, natural enemies in terms of faith, now are spiritual brothers and sisters through Christ's death and resurrection. The new community ethos challenges social customs that grant more worth and value to some groups (slave owners, for example). Other common practices, such as prayer, are redefined and configured to build unity and increase understanding of the characters' new life in Christ. Amidst the daily give and take of growing mature in the faith, characters face hostile spiritual forces that perpetuate evil through individuals and institutions, sowing hostility and strife.

Paul, Author of Ephesians

A central character is the author himself, Paul.[1] He announces himself as an apostle of Jesus Christ in the letter's opening but spends more time describing his current situation. He wants them to know the prayers he makes for them. His pastoral prayers deserve a closer look to discover his concerns and desires for his congregations, so we investigate them in the context of chapter 3. Paul knew the Ephesian congregation from a previous visit, described in Acts 18:19–21; 19:1—20:1. His ministry was characterized by healings and powerful witness, such that many Jews and gentiles held the name of Jesus in high regard (Acts 19:17). He taught in the lecture hall of Tyrannus for over two years, and locals, as well as those passing through Ephesus, had the opportunity to hear his discussions about Christ (Acts 19:9–10).

Paul is in chains, a prisoner for the Lord. Ephesians is one of four letters written while Paul was imprisoned (see also Philippians, Colossians, and Philemon). Yet we should not imagine him incarcerated in a penal system familiar in today's world. His chains held him until a magistrate could decide his case. In Acts, we see the system played out as Paul is interrogated before Governor Felix (Acts 23:26—24:27) and Governor Festus (Acts 25:1–12). Paul likely wrote Ephesians from Rome in ca. 60–62, where he resided in a rented apartment (Acts 28:30). Probably he had some freedom of movement during the day, perhaps going outside to a courtyard. At night, he would be under guard.[2] We will look more closely at Paul's chains in the discussion of chapter 3, but one point should be noted here. The fact that Paul stresses his chains three times (3:1; 4:1; 6:20) increases the likelihood that Paul himself was responsible for the letter, because everyone knew, including Paul, that his life was on the line. He could be put to death for his testimony, and in fact, church tradition states that he was beheaded under Nero's rule.[3] To those who argue that one of Paul's disciples penned this letter after Paul died, I ask: Would a disciple of Paul's write a letter in

1. For a discussion of Pauline authorship, see Cohick, *Ephesians*, 3–25. The claims that Ephesians is a forgery or pseudepigraphy assume we can know an essential Paul and a genuine Pauline letter. Such genuineness is based on the a priori assumption of a center of Paul's thought, for example, justification or apocalyptic eschatology. Often little attention is paid to the role of co-sender or secretary, the specific context of the letter, or the historical setting of the recipients, all of which play a part in the final draft of the letter.

2. Rapske, *Book of Acts and Paul in Roman Custody*, 238.

3. Eusebius, *Hist. eccl.* 2.22.2.

Paul's name and claim for him or herself the honor of being an incipient martyr? The church revered those whose witness led to their death; would a believer include the detail of "chains" as a literary device to increase the credibility of the letter? I find it hard to imagine that a disciple of Paul or any believer would take upon themselves the mantle of incipient martyr to create an illusion of authenticity.

Reasons for Writing Ephesians

The reasons for Paul's letter to the Ephesians are not immediately obvious, as they are in 1 Corinthians or Philippians, for example. Indeed, there is question as to whether Ephesus was the letter's intended city. The latter problem will be addressed first as it impacts the answers to the former. In a few early manuscripts, the designation "in Ephesus" is absent from 1:1.[4] In these cases, the superscription or title page read "to the Ephesians." Several church fathers—including Tertullian, Origen, and Basil the Great—use texts that do not have "in Ephesus" in 1:1.[5] However, all ancient authors (except Marcion) identified our epistle as to the Ephesians. One way to read this omission in a few early manuscripts is that Paul wanted the letter read to numerous churches in the region of Ephesus. The theory postulates that Paul put a deliberate gap in the text, and Tychicus would add the town's name when he arrived there to address the congregation (6:21; see also Col 4:15–16). The theory cannot explain, however, why the preposition "in" was also omitted, nor why the actual manuscripts do not include a gap to

4. The three early witnesses (B א P46) to the omission in the text include "to the Ephesians" in their superscription. The Greek text of P46 reads: τοῖς ἁγίοις οὖσιν καὶ πιστοῖς ἐν Χριστῷ Ἰησοῦ ("to the saints who are and to believers in Christ Jesus"); however the superscription identifying the epistle lists "To the Ephesians." Best, "Ephesians i.1," 29–41 (30), lists the main textual variants:

P - τοῖς ἁγίοις οὖσιν καὶ πιστοῖς P46

B - τοῖς ἁγίοις τοῖς οὖσιν καὶ πιστοῖς א* B* 424c 1739

A - τοῖς ἁγίοις τοῖς οὖσιν ἐν Ἐφέσῳ καὶ πιστοῖς most other manuscripts

5. Tertullian, *Marc.* 5.17.1 (see also 5.11.12); see Best remarks, "it is generally held that Tertullian's accusations relate to the superscription to the letter and not to the text itself: in that case Marcion cannot have had the A text [τοῖς ἁγίοις τοῖς οὖσιν ἐν Ἐφέσῳ καὶ πιστοῖς]; this would also imply that Tertullian did not have 'in Ephesus' in his text." Best, "Ephesians i.1," 30. In his commentary, Origen argues the letter was sent to the Ephesians and explains the absence of the complement "Ephesus" by declaring that Paul emphasized the believers as saints *who are*, connecting this with God's name I AM. See Heine, *Commentaries of Origen and Jerome on St. Paul's Epistle to the Ephesians*, 80. Basil the Great, *Adv. Eunom.* 2.19 [PG 29:612–13].

alert the reader to insert the town's name. Again, if Paul expected this letter to be shared with towns in the region, why not address it to believers in the Lycus Valley or Asia Minor, much as Paul does in his letter to the Galatian churches. A more likely solution is that the omission of "in Ephesus" in 1:1 is a scribal error that was copied in three early Alexandrian manuscripts.

Paul writes to the Ephesians to encourage them, instruct them, and update them on his current situation. From the opening lines to its close, the letter thanks God—Father, Son, and Holy Spirit—for the amazing redemption plan that reveals the mystery of magnanimous mercy, unfailing love, and compassionate kindness. The attitude of thanksgiving offers great encouragement to the Ephesians. The profound theology and aspirational call for discipleship could seem daunting were it not for the constant refrain of God's love that sings through the epistle. The liturgical language woven throughout lends itself to a worship context as instruction in living a life worthy of their calling in Christ is expounded. The unity created by Christ's work on the cross receives extended attention as the marker for mature faith.

Scripture in Ephesians

Paul draws on the Old Testament for instruction and worldview. Although he infrequently quotes the Old Testament in Ephesians, his ideas and teachings are saturated in its message. We see this in his description of what the gentiles missed when they were not part of God's family: excluded from citizenship in Israel, from the covenants, from hope in God (2:12; 3:5–6). As we move through the epistle, in chapter 1 Paul speaks of God placing all things under Christ's feet (1:22), a reference to Ps 8:6 and Ps 110:1. These psalms shaped the earliest Christians' imagination around Christ's lordship, as Peter and the author of Hebrews refer to them (Acts 2:34–35; Heb 2:6–8). Paul refers to this passage in his assurance of God's coming kingdom when Christ has defeated all powers, including death (1 Cor 15:25). Chapter 2 includes an image from Isaiah of the nations coming to Jerusalem, as the gentiles, far from God, now draw near through Christ, our peace (Isa 57:19; Eph 2:12, 17). Chapter 4 draws on Ps 68:18 as Paul describes the gift given by Christ to his body, the church (4:7). Paul cites Ps 4:4 when warning believers against sinning in their anger, urging them to remember they are members of Christ's body (4:26). In chapter 5, Paul cites Gen 2:24 that in marriage the husband and wife, as two people, are made one flesh (5:31).[6] In chapter 6, Paul quotes from the Decalogue that children should obey their parents (6:1–3; Exod 20:12; Deut 5:13–15). Paul also pulls from Isaiah in urging believers to put on the armor of God (Isa 52:7; 59:17).

These quotations and allusions have in common an eschatological focus that God will redeem the world and judge the guilty, making good on his promises. Those promises include ones of inheritance, of covenant keeping, of a people devoted to God, all themes that permeate the Torah, and the Psalms and Isaiah. These promises have been fulfilled in Christ, and the end is near for the full consummation of unity in Christ.

Theology in Ephesians

Several key theological claims are developed in Ephesians, including concentrated attention on the Trinity, Father, the Son, and the Holy Spirit, in creating and executing the redemption plan for humanity (soteriology), and the final cosmic consummation when evil is forever destroyed (eschatology). Another emphasis is the church, described as Christ's body, God's temple, God's family through adoption, a new humanity made up of both Jews and gentiles (ecclesiology).

Turning first to Trinity, Wesley Hill proposes that we understand Trinity as relationship, for we cannot know Father without also knowing Son, for as the Father is eternal, so the Son is eternal. Hill explains, "The *person* 'God'—traditionally referred to as "the Father" in trinitarian discourse—is who he is by virtue of this relation with Jesus ("the Son," in traditional terms); by his act of giving up and raising Jesus . . . God defines himself as a distinct person, in such a way that the relation is internal to the self-definition."[7] Hill notes that both the Father and the Son are called 'Lord' and the identity of the three persons "are constituted in and by their differing ways of relating to one another: God sends and exalts, Jesus is sent and exalted."[8] God the Father is the Father of the Lord Jesus Christ (1:3), the Father of all families (3:15) and of his beloved children (5:1). The Father raised the Son and seated him at his right hand (1:20–21). Jesus Christ is the Son (4:13), the beloved one (1:6), the head of his body, the church (1:22–23), our peace (2:14), the cornerstone (2:20), who gives gifts

6. Ephesians 5:14 could be an allusion to Isa 26:19 and/or 60:1.

7. Hill, *Paul and the Trinity*, 74.

8. Hill, *Paul and the Trinity*, 170.

to his church (4:7, 11), who along with the Father rules the kingdom (5:5). The Holy Spirit is the believer's seal (1:13–14; 4:30) and deposit guaranteeing inheritance in Christ (1:14). The Spirit fills the church (2:22), provides access to the Father (2:18), and fills and strengthens believers' inner life (3:16). Believers can grieve the Holy Spirit by their sinning (4:30). Believers are commanded to be filled with the Holy Spirit as they worship together (5:18).

The three persons work as one in the redemption of humanity and the cosmos. Each person has roles or actions specific to them. To understand the complexity we can use the concept of reduplication, which stresses that when speaking of each person, we must speak of both their essence as God, and their unique properties specific to their person. For example, only the Son became incarnate. Gregory of Nazianzus, a fourth-century theologian, explains "the Three are One from the perspective of their divinity, and the One is Three from the perspective of the properties."[9]

Paul's emphasis on the three persons provides a cosmic depth and breadth to the description of God's salvation plan. Paul can speak about God before time, the immanent Trinity, that created the redemption plan for humanity and the cosmos. Paul can speak about the present time with attention to Christ's work in creating a new humanity, the church, his body, which is strengthened by the Holy Spirit. And he can point to the future, when the Holy Spirit as believers' deposit is fully realized in their inheritance, when all things are unified through Christ. Understanding each divine person's roles brings a clarity and a confidence to believers that their salvation is secure, and the world will be made right at the end. Until then, believers have been made new and are to walk in holiness, together as one family in Christ.

This redemption plan created a new humanity, a new people, the body of Christ. Paul uses two metaphors to help us imagine the church. First, he speaks of this group as Christ's body (1:23; 2:16; 3:6; 4:4, 12; 5:32; see also Rom 12:3–8; 1 Cor 12:27). This body is made up of Jew and gentile, the two become one because of the peace made on the cross (2:14–15). Paul reiterates the importance of this oneness as he describes the mystery of the gospel, which is that, in Christ, gentiles are coheirs and members of the one body and sharers of the promise (3:6). This body is connected to its head, Christ, and is growing and maturing (4:15). Second, he speaks of the

9. Gregory of Nazianzus, *Orations* 31.9, as quoted in Emery, *Trinitarian Theology of St. Thomas Aquinas*, 45. See Hill, *Paul and the Trinity*, 99–103.

church as the temple of God, indwelled by the Holy Spirit and being built up to attain the measure of fullness of Christ (2:21–22; 4:12; see also 1 Cor 3:16; 2 Cor 6:16).

Epistolary Structure in Ephesians

Ephesians' structure divides neatly in half, with the first three chapters focused on God's redemptive plan for all humanity, and the second half concentrating on living the ethics of God's kingdom. One evidence for this structure is the number of imperatives which increases in chapters 4 through 6 to thirty-nine, up from only one in 2:11.[10] This is not to say that Paul does not urge his readers to do or avoid certain thoughts or deeds in the earlier chapters; rather, he builds his case for ethics from a solid theological foundation. Paul lets believers know who they are in Christ, so that they can then live into this new and true identity. In the first three chapters, Paul explains that the forces of darkness were defeated by Christ, but still operate among humans and institutions, so that in the latter three chapters he can reinforce the proper mindset and behaviors that stand firm against the (ultimately defeated) spiritual foes. Paul describes the new family in Christ, adopted and made one new humanity, Jew and gentile, in detail and from several angles in the early chapters, so that he can address behaviors and attitudes proper for members of the kingdom of Christ and of God. The letter starts with the indicative—what is true in Christ—and follows with the imperative—what should be true of believers in Christ. The common theological/ethical thread running through the entire letter is summed up in the phrase "in Christ." Theologically speaking, adoption into God's family and forgiveness of sins depend upon Christ's work on the cross. From the standpoint of ethics, believers' demeanor, their thoughts and actions, form and grow as they mature in Christ.

Paul keeps one eye on the present, daily lives of believers and another eye on the cosmic scene with its malevolent forces and the call to stand firm in the armor of God. Believers themselves put on the new self in Christ and enjoy being seated with Christ in the heavenly places, through God's great mercy and kindness. Everything moves towards the sure promise of all things in heaven and on earth brought into unity in Christ.

See below the outline followed in this commentary.

10. Merkle, *Ephesians*, 111.

EPHESIANS 1

Ephesians 1:1-2: Paul's Greetings

PAUL BEGINS THIS LETTER as he does many others, with the phrase "Paul an apostle of Christ Jesus through the will of God" (2 Cor 1:1; Col 1:1; 2 Tim 1:1). Typically, Paul identifies himself as an apostle (Rom 1:1; 1 Cor 1:1; Gal 1:1). An apostle is a person sent on a mission by another person (2 Cor 8:23; Phil 2:25). To be sent by Christ Jesus is to claim the highest authority for one's mission. It is interesting, therefore, that nowhere else in this letter does Paul refer to himself as an apostle. Instead, he speaks of his imprisonment and identifies himself as an ambassador in chains (3:1; 4:1; 6:20). References to his prisoner status sends a jarring note, but it serves to remove any celebrity prestige from the title "apostle." Paul understands the leadership role of apostle as one of service, helping the church grow to maturity (2:20; 3:5; 4:11). In other letters, Paul further defines his apostolic calling to preach the gospel to gentiles (Gal 1:16; 2:7). This ministry focus comes to the fore in Ephesians with its emphasis on gentiles and Jews becoming one family in the Lord (2:14-16; 3:4-6).

The addressees are identified as a group of holy ones, or saints, and faithful. Paul typically greets his congregations as saints, but he never addresses an individual with that title. Even in this small way, Paul reinforces a key facet of his gospel message, namely, that believers are members of Christ's body, and not simply a collection of individually saved people. The Ephesians are faithful; that is, they are committed to the Lord Jesus and his redemption. The term can also reflect a person's character. For example, Paul praises Tychicus's faithfulness (6:21).

Today we might skim over the second line of Paul's introduction, because he uses it in most of his greetings. We should pause, however, on the theologically rich nouns: grace, peace, Father, Lord. Turning to the first term, grace (*charis*), this term as a wide semantic range in Greek, including (divine) favor, kindness, gift, charitable act, and benefaction. God's gift in Christ is indescribable (2 Cor 9:15, see also 2 Cor 8:9). Paul stresses that this gift is evidence of God's great love and mercy, that activates saving grace (Eph 2:4–5). The second term, peace, is identified with Christ, the one who is our peace (2:14). Just as the grace of God makes alive those who were dead in transgressions (2:5), so too Christ's peace creates one new humanity by the power of the cross (2:14–16).

The third term, Father, refers to God the Father of Jesus Christ, the father of all families (3:14–15) and of all things (4:6), and the father of his children, who are members through Christ of his household (2:19). The Roman emperor claimed the title *pater patriae*, the father of the homeland. The emperor, Octavian Caesar Augustus, was venerated as a son of a god (*divi filius*), as he was the son of the deified Julius Caesar. Paul's description of God the Father contrasts sharply with the imperial ideal. Later Christian creeds speak of God the Father eternally begetting the Son, and Christ the Son as eternally begotten. This language attempts to capture the important distinction between God the Father and human fathers. The Father and Son were always so. There was never a time when the Father did not have the Son; certainly this is something no human father can say. God does not need a consort to create a son, while every human child is born to a mother and father, and both parents equally participate in the creation of this new life. Amy Peeler says it well, "Christians can and should address God, the first person, as 'Father' not because God is male and not because God is more masculine than feminine but because God the Father as an expression of the triune will sent forth his Son *born of a woman*."[1] The Son, the second person of the Trinity, as an expression of the triune will, is incarnated as Mary's son, and the Son of God. His death, resurrection, ascension, and future judgment secures for believers their sure salvation and their new family.

Ephesians 1:3–14: Blessed Be God, Who Blesses Us

Paul starts with God. This rather obvious statement nevertheless holds the key to this passage. Start with God. The overarching message of this passage is God's blessing of salvation, enacted in Christ and sealed with the Holy Spirit, for all by faith to become adopted children of God. Each of the

1. Peeler, *Women and the Gender of God*, 115.

three persons of the Trinity is mentioned as Paul describes the redemption plan that will eventually bring all things into unity in Christ. Daniel Treier speaks of "Scripture's theodramatic ontology [that] begins with the eternal communion between God the Son and God the Father in the love of God the Holy Spirit. Before and outside of earthly time, the life of the Blessed Trinity remains mysterious even with the provision of divine revelation."[2] We know God because of God's self-revelation in his word and the Word. God acts; he chooses, predestines, gives freely, redeems, makes known; all this to demonstrate his grace and love. Humans receive; we are blessed, adopted, chosen, redeemed, forgiven of sins, made aware of the mystery of his will, and marked by the Holy Spirit.

Paul begins before the beginning as he proclaims that God established the salvation plan before the world was formed. The historical moment came with Christ, who brought redemption with his death on the cross. The present age is both broken and being redeemed, ruled by sin and covered in grace. Into this moment God reveals his mystery of grace, that gentiles are co-heirs with Israel, and all are members of one body the church (3:6). Paul stretches his gaze beyond the physical horizon to include the heavens, for the entire cosmos is God's domain. Christ's death set in motion a drawing together in unity all created things, for full redemption is established as all creation rejoices in the wisdom and glory of God. Spiritual authorities look in awe, and some work evil against the church (3:10–11; 6:12).

This passage is a single sentence in Greek, and at 202 words, it is the second longest sentence within Paul's letters behind Colossians 1:9–20. The numerous clauses and additional descriptions elevate the majesty of the blessing. We will step through the grammar and syntax and return to examine key terms.

One way into Paul's argument is to focus on the verbs and participles. The main finite verb is "chose" (1:4), whose subject is God, the Father of our Lord Jesus Christ. God chose us, Paul declares, the Ephesian believers and all believers. Other finite verbs within clauses draw out the implications of God choosing this plan of salvation. God freely gives his grace in Christ (1:6). Indeed, he lavishes it (1:8). Additionally, God purposed (1:9) his plan of redemption in Christ, and that plan will bring all things into unity in Christ (1:10). Once more we read that God "chose" us in Christ (1:11), and in both cases, this verb is followed by the participle "predestined." Later theological discussions used predestination as a theological category, but

2. Treier, *Lord Jesus Christ*, 49.

here, Paul speaks specifically about that to which one is predestined, namely adoption into God's family (1:5). This adoption entails an inheritance as a member of God's family (1:14).

A second approach to understand this complex passage is to focus on pronouns and repeated phrases, for both emphasize Christ's work in relation to God's glory. Several relative pronouns stress what we have "in him," including having redemption (1:7), being chosen (1:11), and being included and sealed (1:13–14). Paul regularly speaks of believers being "in Christ," as participating in Christ's life, and in this section, every verse but 1:8 and 1:14 mentions being in Christ or God working through Christ. Throughout Ephesians, we find "in him" expanded with other metaphors, such as putting on the new self (4:24). The focus on being in Christ is captured in the terms "cruciformity"[3] and "christoformity."[4] Both terms emphasize the disciple's call to be like Jesus, to serve and not be served, to love generously, and to walk humbly. Paul puts it to the Corinthians this way: imitate me as I imitate Christ (1 Cor 11:1). Three times in our passage, Paul breaks forth in praise of God's glory (1:6, 12, 14). The context is God's plan of redemption that creates adopted children, Jew and gentile, both now redeemed in Christ.

A third approach to grasp Paul's argument is to follow the actions of God the Father, Son, and Holy Spirit in this lengthy sentence. Paul focuses on God the Father of Jesus Christ and the father of all people (3:14) who determined, before humans and all creation came into being, that redemption will be accomplished in the Son, the beloved (see also Matt 3:17). Not only forgiveness of sins, but God created a family of co-heirs with the Son, through adoption through the Son. Paul then turns his attention to the Son, who is named as Christ or with a pronoun in ten of these twelve verses. Christ's work launched the countdown towards unity of all things in earth and heaven. Said another way, the cross and resurrection achieve an individual's forgiveness of their sins and at the same time set cosmic forces in motion towards unity. Finally, Paul celebrates the Holy Spirit's work in each believer, securing their inheritance in the people of God. Paul speaks of believers being sealed, much as someone would use a wax seal to declare their ownership of the item. However, in this case, it is not an external bit of wax, but the indwelling Holy Spirit who marks the one who puts their hope in Christ.

3. Gorman, *Cruciformity*; Gorman, *Inhabiting the Cruciform God.*

4. McKnight, *Pastor Paul.*

Having laid out the work of God in redemption, we must pay attention to Paul's description of the faithful follower, the recipient of God's abundant blessings. A believer is chosen—not to "be saved" in some static sense, but to be "in him [Christ]" and to be holy and blameless, a condition fully possible only in Christ (see also 5:27). A believer is predestined as God acts to draw the believer into relationship as a child with God the Father through Christ. Paul relates a similar idea to the Romans as he declares that those God foreknew, he predestined to be conformed to the image of the Son. Those predestined know that they are now members of God's family, co-heirs with Christ. They are predestined to be in God's family (Rom 8:16–17; 29–30). The theme of inheritance is repeated at the end of the passage, reinforcing the reality that believers are members of God's household.

Ephesians 1:3–6

The long passage will be analyzed in segments, and we turn first to 1:3–6, where the focus is on God the Father choosing believers in Christ to be holy and choosing to adopt them as his children. The segment begins and ends with Paul's repeated use of "praise" as he contemplates the amazing salvation plan of God. God's character is to bless, and God has done so beyond all comprehension by giving believers all blessings in Christ. Paul includes himself here as one of "us" who receives such blessings and thus extols the Lord.

In 1:4, Paul writes that God chose, and Paul will explain when and what he chose, what resulted from the choice, and why God made the choice. The verb "to choose" is the main or finite verb of this lengthy passage, and we discover that God chose the redemption plan for his world before the dawn of time. Paul's point is that the overwhelming love expressed in this plan was *always* in the mind of God and was not a quickly thrown together rescue operation to save humanity and creation after Adam's sin created the crisis. The plan chosen was implemented through the Son, Jesus Christ. The focus is on God choosing a plan of salvation; Paul does not concentrate on whether God chose specific individuals. God chose to create a people holy and blameless, in a highly qualified, creaturely manner, resembling God's own holiness (see also 5:27). He chose to create a people unto himself, a family of adopted sons and daughters, of which he would be Father.

The phrase "in love" in 1:5 probably connects with the participle "he predestined." Who and for what did God predestine? Paul states that

God predestined believers to be adopted into God's family through the Son, Jesus Christ. It is difficult to determine whether Paul imagines both the choosing and predestining to happen sequentially or simultaneously. Perhaps Paul reflects that the choosing was done by means of predestining. Paul repeats the participle "predestined" later in this passage (1:11), yet the verb's meaning here is likewise debated. The overarching sense one gets with this verb twice repeated is God's independence from any human involvement in creating or implementing the plan. Paul expresses a similar idea to the Romans when he writes that God foreknew and predestined believers to be conformed to the image of his Son (Rom 8:29). Paul continues that those predestined were also called, justified, and glorified (Rom 8:30). All this so that the Son would be the firstborn among many (Rom 8:29).

Not only is there a link between Romans and Ephesians with the verb "predestined," but also we find in both places a discussion about adoption (see also Gal 4:5). In Romans, Paul explains that those who have the Holy Spirit are adopted members of God's family and can call God "*Abba*, Father" (Rom 8:15; see also 8:23). This adoption is secure in that the Spirit testifies in our hearts that we are God's children, but our full adoption is achieved at the resurrection, the redemption of our bodies (Rom 8:23). Adoption was practiced widely among Romans. Perhaps the most famous example is that of Julius Caesar adopting Octavian, who later became the first emperor. It was much less common to adopt a young female of any age, for they could be incorporated into the family through marriage. The adopted son might have a living father who would agree to the adoption because it would provide a better situation for his son. And the adopting father might have a birth son that is disinherited by the adopted son, based on the perceived superiority of the latter. While Jews were familiar with the practice, they rarely used adoption in their own families. The Old Testament stresses God's provision of children as one way God sustains Israel. Moreover, God speaks of Israel as his son, emphasizing the relationship between God and his people.

Paul's focus on adoption broadens the scope of Christ's redemptive work to include creating a new family whose members are each forgiven and deeply loved. I stress the family aspect of salvation because of the highly individualized society that many live in today. In Paul's world, people based their self-understanding and identity on their status within their family and the wider community. Paul's emphasis on adoption, especially to slaves and the very poor, would have sounded incredible, perhaps too good to be true.

Paul insists that in fact all believers in Christ share equally as members of God's family, now and when they receive the final inheritance.

God bestows his favor on humanity through giving grace in Christ (1:6). The term "grace" and the term "gift" are one and the same in Greek (*charis*). The related verb used here captures the benevolent gesture of God, which Paul further describes as abundant and overflowing (1:8). Paul stresses that believers receive this freely given, overflowing, richly abundant grace.

One final point about the recipients of God's grace, they come from two people groups: Jews and gentiles. Paul inherited these categories based on the religious distinctions of these groups. Jews followed the one true God, and gentiles were pagans, following false gods. Of course, Paul knew gentiles who were attracted to Judaism and who frequented the synagogue, for example Lydia in Philippi (Acts 16:11–40). These God-fearers were an important group in the early church, for they were eager to hear more about Jesus the Messiah of God. Paul alludes to Jews and gentiles at the end of this passage in his "us" and "you" references. Paul declares that "we" were the first to put our hope in Christ (1:13), and by "we" he means those Jews who followed Jesus in his ministry and after his resurrection. Then Paul turns to the Ephesians, most of whom are gentiles, and stated that "you all" also believed and are now included in Christ. We must pay attention to these two people groups, for if we ignore them, Paul's argument later in chapter 2 loses much of its power. If we overlook the reality of gentile believers, we cannot fully understand and appreciate the power of Christ our peace (2:14) and the greatness of his work in creating one new humanity (2:15).

Ephesians 1:7–12

The second section of this lengthy passage includes 1:7–12, with its focus on Christ's work on the cross and its ultimate end to bring all things into unity in Christ. Paul emphasizes "in Christ" or "in him" throughout these four verses as he explains the salvation plan. In 1:7–8, Paul speaks of redemption and forgiveness. The first term, "redemption," is a common theological term today, but is rarely used in the New Testament; three of its ten appearances occur in our epistle. The noun carries the sense of deliverance for a prisoner or a kidnapped victim. In the Old Testament, it carries a cultic meaning with the half-shekel tax (Exod 30:11–16). Jesus picks up this meaning when he describes his death as a ransom for many (Matt 20:28;

Mark 10:45). Paul uses the term as he describes God's grace in providing redemption in Christ (Rom 3:24), adding that this comes at the shedding of his blood (3:25), ideas linked here in Ephesians. Later in Romans, Paul uses "redemption" as he speaks about believers' adoption (8:23), a crucial concept related to God's work in Christ. Here in Ephesians, Paul continues his explanation on redemption by linking it with forgiveness of sins, through Christ's death on the cross, although he does not use the term "cross" but rather speaks of his shed blood (1:7; see also Acts 20:28).

The second term, forgiveness, is used infrequently in the New Testament epistles, but more commonly in the Gospels and Acts. Paul attributes the redemption and forgiveness to God's riches of grace. Paul celebrates such riches five times throughout Ephesians as he speaks of forgiveness (1:7), believers' inheritance (1:18), God's kindness (2:7), God's glory (3:16), and the riches of Christ (3:8). Paul continues in 1:8 that these riches of redemption are lavished on believers, and one has the sense of abandoned generosity based on an unending source of grace.

Paul continues his description of the work of Christ, now with two additional concepts that feature prominently in the epistle, namely, mystery and unity. Looking first at "mystery," we think of a riddle to be solved or a whodunit thriller. But Paul speaks here of the magnificent plan of God to redeem the world that exceeds any human imagination or capacity to achieve. The mystery's content centers on Christ's redemption. Paul will be more specific in chapter 3, explaining the mystery as the creation of a new people, Jew and gentile, through Christ into one body (3:6; see also 5:32). The second term, *unity*, fits tightly with "mystery." The unity highlighted here is cosmic in scope, extending to all things on earth and in heaven. There is a reconciliation, a renewal of all that is dead, and the fixing of all that is broken in God's creation. Paul stresses the scope of God's power and goodness. Recall that in 1:4 Paul spoke of things that happened before the world was founded, and now he speaks of the culmination of God's creative work. God is not defeated by sin and death, nor does he abandon his good creation. Elsewhere Paul speaks of God's judgment against sin (2:1; 5:5), so this unity of all things includes the execution of his justice. God brings all things into unity, through Christ, thereby demonstrating his all-sufficient power to rectify all things, and his super-abundant love that desires this perfected unity.

Paul describes this summing up of all things in Christ with a verb that can be translated as "to sum up" (*anakephalaioō*). Elsewhere, Paul describes the summing up of all the commandments with this verb (Rom 13:9). The related noun (*kephalaion*) carries a similar sense of summing up the author's key point (Heb 8:1). Frank Thielman explains the difficulty in interpreting this rare verb. He notes that some interpreters focus on the prefix *"ana"* which is similar to "re" in English. Paul's thought was later captured by the doctrine of recapitulation, which is prominent in certain church fathers. Irenaeus emphasizes that Christ in his incarnation took up Adam's plight so that he might redeem humanity and restore it to its pre-fall image and likeness of God. As Michael Bird explains the doctrine, "Jesus recapitulated in his person all that Adam should have been."[5] Thielman remarks that the verb's meaning is incorporated in the prefix and thus was not used to speak about restoration, but about summarizing that which had been argued. A second false step is to define the term based on what comes later in our epistle. Those who know a bit of Greek might think that the verb is related to the term for head, *kephalē*. However, the noun *kephalaion* and the verb *kephalaioō* are cognate to the verb in 1:10. The noun and verb both have the idea of summing up something in an argument. Thielman concludes Paul stresses here that "God will use Christ to bring together the disparate elements of creation."[6] It is the cosmic dimension of salvation that Paul has in view and will elaborate upon in the second half of the chapter.

Having provided the cosmic viewpoint of Christ's work, Paul focuses more narrowly on believers' inheritance. In 1:11, Paul uses a verb typically translated as "appointed by lot" (*klēroō*) to reiterate that believers are heirs in Christ (1:11), for the context suggests that Paul has in mind believers' inheritance in Christ. Paul uses the noun "inheritance" in 1:18, but he has already declared that God's plan includes adoption, implying the creation of heirs (1:5; see also Col 1:12). Paul repeats the verb "to predestine" (see 1:5), reiterating God's work in achieving his purpose to redeem humanity and bring unity to the cosmos in Christ.

Ephesians 1:12–14

Turning to the final section of this lengthy, awe-inspiring passage, Paul continues to stress the surpassing greatness of God's salvation plan, which results in praise of his glory. While there is no question as to the ultimate meaning, interpreters puzzle over two issues in 1:12, namely the use of the

5. Bird, *Evangelical Theology*, 442.

6. Thielman, *Ephesians*, 65–67.

third person plural pronoun "we" and the unique verb "first to put hope." Looking first at the pronoun, a comparison is made between "we" and "you" in 1:13. One possibility is that Paul is thinking about the timing of hearing the gospel message, that he and other Jews were the first to trust in Christ, and later, the gentile believers in Ephesus heard and received the word of grace. Paul stresses the distinctions between Jew and gentile in the remaining chapters, so it is plausible he begins to do so here. Another possibility is that Paul's argument revolves around the current age and the age to come, with "we" signalling the present age of grace, with the implication that full consummation will occur when all things are united in Christ. The reference in 1:13 to "you" listeners in Ephesus is Paul's attempt to reassure his congregation that their hope is secure, that his description of God's salvation plan, outlined in the preceding verses, is secure.

Paul insists that believers put their hope in Christ. He speaks of we who were the first to put our hope in Christ, and this verb is unique to the New Testament. The perfect tense of the participle indicates a past act that has ongoing impact in the present. Hope is an important feature of Paul's gospel message. In his prayer at the end of this chapter, Paul asks God to give the Ephesians a better understanding of the hope of their calling and of their glorious inheritance (1:18). They are called to one hope (4:4) from their situation of no hope before they knew Christ (2:12). In this term, we see Paul's eschatology, a conviction that believers have all they need now for a holy and blameless life in Christ and will enjoy perfect unity with God and others in the age to come when all things are summed up in Christ.

Paul closes his lengthy benediction that began in 1:3 with an emphasis on the believer's inheritance through Christ. The Holy Spirit plays a leading role now in assuring believers that their salvation is secure. They heard and believed, and so are sealed with the Holy Spirit. The seal authenticates ownership; it identifies the object as approved. Paul uses the concept when he speaks of Abraham's circumcision as a seal (Rom 4:11). The believers' seal of the Holy Spirit not only establishes that they are God's, but also that God has claimed them as his own. The Spirit's seal marks them publicly as members of God's family, and this seal will be evidence on the day when redemption is accomplished (4:30; see 2 Cor 5:5). Paul explains that the Holy Spirit's presence in their lives acts as a down payment for their eternal life to come. Paul expresses a similar thought to the Corinthians as Paul stresses God's faithfulness to his promises (2 Cor 1:22). Paul explains that believers' redemption is guaranteed by the presence, the deposit, of Holy Spirit.

The Holy Spirit of God, the third person of the Trinity, animates the life of faithful living now, giving believers a taste of what is to come. Believers are redeemed by Christ's work on the cross (1:7) and are kept safe or preserved until the full consummation of that redemption (1:14).

Ephesians 1:3–14: Reflections for Preaching and Teaching

In our passage, Paul presents a thirty-thousand-foot view of God's salvation plan. We push above the clouds, now seeing the tops of mountains, the patchwork of farmers' fields, oceans, or deserts stretching to the horizon. From my window seat, I feel a sense of awe, of majesty, that the Creator God made such magnificence. And I feel small, buckled in a silver bullet racing through the air, needing the speed to stay at that height, vulnerable to un-seen jet streams. Paul wants us to see the vastness of God's salvation plan, but he also wants us to feel safe, for we are part of God's family, in Christ. These two major ideas—majesty and intimacy—permeate the passage. We are deeply, wholly loved by God, and we are but one part of a universe being made right and whole, holy, by the Father, through the Son, attended by the Holy Spirit. Both are true absolutely and fully at all times. Such salvation offers comfort to individual believers that, on the one hand, salvation is all about "me," and at the same time, salvation is so much bigger and greater than me. We are loved beyond measure and part of a measureless reality that takes up all that is known and yet to be known. At any given moment, preachers today might stress one or other of these central truths, but one should return to the other, so that believers grow to see their faith secure in the majestic, intimate salvation plan established through Christ Jesus.

It is interesting that Paul first stresses the believer's holiness and adop-tion (1:4–5) before mentioning forgiveness of sins (1:7). We might expect him to lead with forgiveness of sins, based on our modern emphasis on the individual and individualism. While Paul is certainly not naïve about the dangers and damages of sin and sins, his approach to that problem has much to do with his emphasis on the church and its holy witness to the wider world. Moreover, the individual is best understood as part of a group, at the very least, one of a pair—they are paired with Christ, co-heirs with him, and thus with other co-heirs. One's relationship with God, therefore, is not only restored through forgiveness of sins, but also by the adoption of the forgiven one into the family.

What would be the expectations of the Ephesians on receiving the gift of grace from such an exalted Benefactor? Today, we praise a gift that has "no strings attached," for that signals a disinterested, altruistic giver. But in the ancient world, gifts were given to create and sustain relationships. John Barclay, in his work *Paul and the Gift*, explores in detail the dynamics around gift-giving and maps Paul's explanations of God's gift giving onto the cultural expectations.[7] He concludes that in two areas, gift-giving in the ancient world differed from our own expectations today in the West. First, in the ancient world, gifts were given to worthy recipients, while Paul stresses that God's gift of grace is given to unworthy people. The ancient world's gift-giver would not want to waste valuable resources on a dissolute or unproductive person. We do this today when we give grants and scholarships to students—typically we offer them to those students we believe will make the most of their education. Paul insists, however, that God does not look at the person's capacities; he does not weigh the possible merits nor the person's potential. God gives his grace to those who are unworthy, period.

Most gentiles and Jews would assume that God gives the gift of grace to those who deserve it or who might eventually deserve it. The gentile believers had to reject their culture's view that gifts are only given to worthy recipients. Jewish believers carried some of these assumptions as well; Jesus's disciples were amazed at his words that it is hard for a rich person to be saved (Matt 19:16–30; Mark 10:17–31).[8] Yet Paul is clear that God's grace is no respecter of persons. God's wisdom is unlike human wisdom, for God gives his grace to those who might never show by their actions that God chose the wise, just, and beautiful people (1 Cor 1:26—2:7). God's gift is unconditioned; there is no intrinsic social worth that God sees in making grace available; rather, it is God's immeasurable love that finds expression in this lavish display of grace.

Second, Barclay's research shows that a gift in the ancient world brought together two people or groups. The gift started or maintained a relationship. This meant that the recipient expected to have obligations to their benefactor, and such obligations were not understood as onerous but would create relationship. We could say that there were strings attached to the gift. This sounds negative to our ear, but only because we have a

---

7. Barclay, *Paul and the Gift*.

8. Barclay contends, "Paul opposes those who think Torah-observance is the essential expression of faith not because 'law' or 'works' are problematic principles of soteriology, but because the Torah—like every other pre-constituted norm—has been dethroned as a criterion of worth by the unconditioned gift of Christ." Barclay, *Paul and the Gift*, 567–68.

preconceived idea that a gift should be given in a disinterested manner. God, however, is very interested in creating relationships with his creation, with humans.

Based on Barclay's research, our language about receiving God's grace can be sharpened to reflect better Paul's teaching. When we speak about God's unconditional grace, we must hold together the unconditionality of its offer—there are no prior conditions, for all are unworthy to receive it— and its conditionality that draws us into relationship, into Christ's own life that lives now in us (see also Gal 2:20). Barclay rightly declares that Paul's understanding of God's grace is that it is "given without regard to worth."[9]

Teaching on the Trinity is not for the fainthearted, but understanding the basics can steer congregations away from doctrinal ditches. One aspect that presents conceptual difficulties surrounds the eternal generation of the Son from the Father. The Nicene Creed states, "We believe in one Lord, Jesus Christ, eternally begotten of the Father; God from God, light from light . . . begotten not made, of one being [*homoousios*] with the Father." Several theological ramifications come from this declaration. First, Father and Son are proper names, and through metaphor and analogy, help us understand God better, and distinguish human family and finitude from God's life within God's Self. Second, the proper names help us understand that these eternal persons are related to each other; said another way, they are in relationship within God's life. Third, Treier stresses the classical position that "both the divine essence and the divine will are one, with no hint of ontological subordination."[10] This means that when Scripture speaks of Jesus's obedience to the Father, it refers to the hypostatic union of divine and human which is the mystery of the incarnation. The Son and the Father have one will, for they are one God in three persons. To make a crass analogy, we should not imagine that God the Father ordered Jesus his Son down to earth to do a dirty job, much as a human father might order his son to take out the trash. Treier elegantly summarizes the immanent Trinity and the redemptive plan of God where "the Father initiates, the Son effects, and the Spirit perfects; correspondingly, only the Son assumed human flesh. Yet appropriation must never obscure the perichoretic—mutually interwoven—being of the three persons; we must also say that 'God became incarnate,' for the incarnation is an inseparable operation of the Blessed

9. Barclay, *Paul and the Gift*, 6.
10. Treier, *Lord Jesus Christ*, 60.

Trinity."[11] Fourth, the emphasis on eternal generation invites humans to participate in this divine relationship of love, through the redemptive plan of God established through Christ for our adoption.

Ephesians 1:15–23: Christ Is Head of His Body, the Church

Paul typically begins his letters with a thanksgiving, but in Ephesians, the thanksgiving follows a lengthy praise to God for the incredible blessings bestowed on believers. Key themes such as inheritance and God's glory continue to ring out, but now are joined by notes of God's power and of believers knowing God better. Paul continues to operate within chronological and spatial frameworks, stressing the present and the coming age, and the material and the spiritual realities on earth and in heaven. And a new metaphor emerges, the church as Christ's body, which Paul nuances in several ways as he drives home the mysterious, marvelous truth that believers are members of Christ's body (5:30).

Paul offers thanks to God for the Ephesians, specifically their faith in Jesus the Messiah and their love for other believers. While these two characteristics should follow as night the day, Paul knew that not all who genuinely confessed belief in the gospel message loved others who did the same. To the Philippians, he talks about those who preached Christ out of envy and rivalry against Paul, taking advantage of his imprisonment (Phil 1:15–18). Again, to the Philippians, he enjoins two of his co-workers, Euodia and Syntyche, to be unified in their ministries, be of the same mind as they co-labor for the Lord (4:2–3). The lack of love for others in Corinth, manifested in their factions and in creating celebrity apostles ("I follow Cephas!" "I follow Apollos!"), brought out a strong admonition from Paul. He warned that flashy, fancy rhetoric that orators pass off as truth can empty the cross of its power (1 Cor 1:17).

Later in their history, the Ephesian church will lose their first love. The letter to the angel of the church in Ephesus that we find in the book of Revelation warns this church that they have forsaken or moved away from their first love (Rev 2:4). The Ephesians are in danger of having the lampstand removed, having their church collapse. While they are praised for resisting false teachings, and for persevering in their beliefs in a difficult, even hostile pagan environment, nevertheless, without love, their deeds come to nothing. What was this first love? Perhaps it is this love of other believers

11. Treier, *Lord Jesus Christ*, 61.

that Paul notes here. We cannot be sure what replaced their first love, but I wonder if it became a toxic self-love that grew arrogant at its good deeds and righteous knowledge.

We are in the realm of speculation, but this question becomes important as we turn now to Paul's prayer, for this prayer asks that the Ephesians understand more fully what their inheritance involves. The prayer asks for more wisdom, revelation, enlightenment, and power. Used without love, these become dangerous to believers and the church. Therefore, we cannot assume that Paul's thanksgiving for their love of the brethren is a throwaway line or unimportant. In fact, it is bedrock on which the prayer builds.

Ephesians 1:15–19

Paul addresses God, who is identified as the God of the Lord Jesus Christ and as the glorious Father or Father of glory. Earlier, Paul described God as the Father of the Lord Jesus Christ (1:3); here this idea is expanded a bit, and Paul will declare that God is the father of all people (3:14). Here and in chapter 3, the context is prayer. This context reinforces the overarching theme that believers are members of God's household. As such, they can ask their Father for good gifts and expect that God will wisely give them what they need and bless them out of his abundant riches in Christ. Lest we think Paul promotes here a "health and wealth" gospel, let us remember that Paul writes this epistle while in chains for Christ. Suffering is the expected lot of the believer, as they imitate their suffering savior.

Paul asks that God would give the Ephesians several things. First, a spirit of wisdom and revelation that leads to greater understanding of God. Second, that he would give to them enlightenment in their mind's eye to better see the fullness of their reality in Christ. This reality includes the hope of the calling, the riches of the inheritance, and the greatness of God's power in believers. Looking at each in turn, Paul first asks that believers are given a spirit of wisdom. Most likely Paul refers to the Holy Spirit here, for three reasons. First, when he speaks of a person's own spirit, he makes it clear, as he does in the phrase "spirit of your mind" (4:23; see also Rom 8:15; 1 Cor 4:21). Second, Paul does not always use the definite article ("the") when speaking of the Holy Spirit (see Rom 8:4, 5). Third, Paul speaks of revelation, which is not something the human mind can discern (see 3:3–5). Paul's request does not imply that the Ephesians currently lack the Holy Spirit within them now, for Paul has already stated emphatically that believers are sealed with the Spirit as a marker of their inheritance as a child of God. Instead, Paul wants them to know God more deeply and completely. The focus is relationship, not doctrinal beliefs, as important as the latter are. But recalling the opening thanksgiving that praised their love for God's people, we see Paul's continuing emphasis on God's love for us, our love for others, and now our understanding of both.

The second request is that believers will more accurately comprehend their place in God's family. Paul stated earlier that anyone who hears the message of truth and accepts it by faith, receives the Spirit (1:13), but this first step is only the start of an ongoing relationship that offers greater and greater depth of insight. Perhaps this analogy helps: on the wedding day, a new relationship begins as the two become one flesh (Gen 2:24; quoted in Eph 5:31). The subsequent marriage provides opportunities to grow in that relationship. So too here in Paul's prayer, the believer has the Holy Spirit from their first day in the faith and has the opportunity and joy to explore more deeply all that this relationship offers.

Three specific aspects of this relationship are highlighted by Paul. First, Paul desires that believers embrace with confidence the hope they have in God. Such hope does not disappoint because it is rooted in God's actions (Rom 8:24–25). Paul describes it with the language of invitation, reinforcing the sense that it is God who acts to create and sustain our relationship with him (Eph 4:1, 4). Second, and relatedly, Paul asks that they know their inheritance more fully and embrace the riches of its glory. Said another way, Paul asks that God give them a godly imagination to plumb the depths of their true worth as children of God. Paul knows that perhaps 20 percent of those believers listening in Ephesus are slaves; they have no social worth in the world's eyes, and no inheritance, for they have no family. What about on the other end of the social ladder? Paul wants every mind renewed and enlightened as to their proper worth in God's sight and not based on their social worth—great or meager—which is doled out by society.

Third and finally, Paul asks God that believers know the power of God. Paul will describe this power further, and as he does, he slides from his prayer into a celebration of God's resurrection power and the rule of Christ over all things. Paul recognizes God's unsurpassed power and makes the implicit claim that this power is used only and always for good. The power is that which raised Christ. Christ's death granted forgiveness of sins (1:7), and his resurrection defeated death, for he is the first fruits, and his followers will also experience resurrection life (1 Cor 15:20–24).

Ephesians 1:19–23

As Paul moves from his prayer to further describing God's power, he speaks of Christ's resurrection and ascension. Not only is Christ raised from the dead, but he is seated at God's right hand (see also 1 Pet 3:22). To be placed at a person's right hand indicates the bestowal of great honor. James and John's request to sit at the right and left hands of Jesus in his kingdom draw on this custom. Jesus rebukes them as not understanding the true nature of this kingdom. Jesus asks if they can drink the cup of suffering that he will drink (Mark 10:35–45). God the Father honors God the Son, who in his incarnation—with his birth, ministry, death, and resurrection—was obedient to death on a cross (Phil 2:8; Heb 5:8–9). We must always remember that honor in God's kingdom is based on doing good works (2:10), giving self-sacrificially, and blessing others out of obedience to God.

Jesus continues to exist in his glorified body, the one which appeared to many disciples and continues to intercede for believers. The believers' confident hope in a raised and glorified body depends on Christ retaining his glorified bodily existence, for our life is maintained only in his life. Paul draws on Ps 110:1, wherein "the LORD says to my lord: 'Sit at my right hand until I make your enemies a footstool for your feet'" (Ps 110:1 NIV 2011; see also Ps 8:6). The early church viewed this psalm through messianic lens (see Matt 22:43–45; Luke 20:41–44; Heb 1:13).

When Paul states that everything is put under Christ's feet, he especially includes death, which is also in view in 1 Cor 15:12–58. Christ has been exalted above all other powers, evil and good, present and future, human and spiritual forces. Today, we have a horrific image of the boot on the neck, which typifies domination and abuse of power, and in the United States, it manifests in racism and white supremacy. Paul is not creating that picture with his allusion but is assuring the Ephesians that nothing is so powerful as to take away the redemption gained in Christ. Jesus spoke against imagining power as spectacular contests against evil. Two poignant examples come to mind. First, in Luke's Gospel, the disciples return from their missional tour overjoyed that even demons were obedient to Jesus's name. Jesus was unimpressed and refocused them on the fact that their names are written in heaven (Luke 10:17–20). Second, in the Sermon on the Mount, Jesus warns against those "disciples" who do great miracles and exorcisms but do not understand him. Jesus will say to them that he never knew them, and they will be sent away (Matt 7:22–23).

Paul uses the image of enemies under Christ's feet and continues the metaphor by using another body part: the head. God raised Christ to be seated at his right hand, thus all other powers are below him in terms of honor and strength, goodness and holiness. So too God gave Christ to the church. Some translations use "appoint" rather than "gave," but the verb (*didōmi*) does not carry the former meaning in other contexts. Paul speaks of Christ and head, and the question is how the term "head" relates to Christ. Is it a predicate accusative, to be translated as "Christ as head"? Or is it in apposition to "church"? An observation might help answer this. Paul uses the phrase "over all things" and this likely refers to "head," since we have already determined that *didōmi* is best translated as "to give." That would mean that "head" is a predicate: "Christ as head over all things, to the church." The church, in other words, is not under Christ's feet, but is his body. The church need not fear any power or authority, for all are under Christ, and the believer is in Christ, a member of Christ's body.

The term "head" carries the figurative meaning of leader in both Hebrew and English. But it is not the case in Greek (*kephalē*). The Greek dictionary, Liddell and Scott, from 1843, did not offer "leader" as one of its more than twenty-five entries. From the first century, Seneca described the emperor Nero as head of the empire, and he explains that the head is the source of human wellness for the body, so too Nero should rule in such a way as to bring health to his people (*De clementia* 2.2.1).[12] This leads some exegetes to use "source" as a translation.[13]

Others find a few places where *kephalē* could refer to leader or authority. Wayne Grudem researched 2,336 examples of the noun in ancient sources, and concluded that in the vast majority of uses, *kephalē* referred to the physical head.[14] About 5 percent of the time, it was used metaphorically, and 3 percent of the time, the noun indicated a starting point or top. In only 2 percent of cases did *kephalē* indicate leader or authority. The 2 percent

12. For a discussion, see Thiselton, *First Epistle to the Corinthians*, 816–17.

13. Mickelsen and Mickelsen, "What Does *kephalē* Mean in the New Testament?," 98–99, 105–10. See also Fee, who states that the translators of the LXX, "who ordinarily used *kephalē* to translate *rōš* when the physical 'head' was intended, almost never did so when 'ruler' was intended, thus indicating that this metaphorical sense is an exceptional usage and not part of the ordinary range of meanings for the Greek word." Fee, *First Epistle to the Corinthians*, 502–3.

14. Grudem, "Does *kephalē* ('Head') Mean 'Source' or 'Authority Over' in Greek Literature?," 38–59; Grudem, "Meaning of *kephalē* ('Head')," 25–65.

included material translated from Hebrew (where the term can mean leader); such examples from Hebrew are therefore not relevant to the question.

A better understanding would be to see *kephalē* as part of the creative metaphor Paul develops with "feet" and with "body." Interpreters following this path suggest *kephalē* is a synecdoche of the whole, standing for the entire body,[15] or as the preeminent part of the body.[16] The position of preeminence is found in the patronage system, with patrons providing a benefit, and clients reciprocating by offering honor. Cynthia Westfall concludes, "Functioning as a 'head' may be the grounds for holding a position of authority over a client, but it is not the same thing as the exercise of authority."[17] Additionally, Michelle Lee-Barnewall observes that when the metaphor is used in the context of politics or military, the emphasis is on a soldier protecting his head, and by extension, the emperor should be protected because he has primary place in the community. She highlights that the assumption would be for the body to sacrifice itself for its head, and remarks at the gospel paradox where the head sacrifices for his body.[18]

Paul uses the metaphor of the church, *ekklēsia*, as the body of Christ extensively in Ephesians. Paul uses the typical Greek term for assembly, *ekklēsia*, and infuses it with gospel meaning. This assembly is a living body, it is a temple (2:21), it is God's household (2:19). Paul stresses its newness, created by Christ who is our peace (2:14–15). Paul encourages its growth, as he asks that every believer together grow up into maturity (4:16). He commands husbands to love their wives as their own bodies, emphasizing the oneness within marriage that mysteriously reflects the union of Christ and his body (Eph 5:29–30). Church is a community that meets regularly to celebrate their life in Christ. Unlike other *ekklēsiai* in Paul's day, the church's main allegiance was to Christ, and thus its members were drawn from across society. Meeting weekly, the community of believers often shared a meal as they worshiped. The believers practiced communion and baptism as their ancient rites of entering and maintaining fellowship as family members in

---

15. Thiselton, *First Epistle to the Corinthians*, 812–22.

16. Thiselton, *First Epistle to the Corinthians*, 812–22. Westfall, *Paul and Gender*, examines *kephalē* in the context of reciprocity and family structures, noting that the English term "head" does not carry the same semantic range as the Greek κεφαλή. In the case of 1 Cor 11:3, Westfall argues that Paul "has drawn the metaphor of the man being woman's head from the language of kinship." Westfall, *Paul and Gender*, 40.

17. Westfall, "'This Is a Great Metaphor!,'" 587.

18. Lee-Barnewall, *Neither Complementarian Nor Egalitarian*, 229–39; Lee-Barnewall, "Turning ΚΕΦΑΛΗ on Its Head," 608.

God's household. Paul describes believers as filled with the Holy Spirit, and singing hymns, making music, giving thanks to God, and submitting to each other based on their reverence for Christ (5:18–21).

In the final verse of this chapter, Paul states that the church is Christ's body. Paul has established that Christ has all powers and authorities in submission under his feet and that he is head over all these powers. But the rulers and authorities are not part of Christ's body. He is head of the body, his church, to which he is united in an inseparable way. This union does not mean that the church is equal to Christ or that it is the incarnation of Christ now. The incarnation was a singular event, and Jesus has his own raised body (1:20; 1 Cor 15:20). Instead, the metaphor of head and body invites an image of a growing, organic entity.

Ephesians 1:15–23: Reflections for Preaching and Teaching

Christ raised from the dead. This is the central idea of this passage and invites us to face head-on the reality of death. Ironically, this beautiful, inspiring passage is to be read against the black background of death. It is death that breaks all hope, all tomorrows. Death that comes suddenly or not fast enough. Death that creates immobilizing fear and desperate grief. And yet, it is death that activates an inheritance for the person's heirs. Death that brings a new chapter beyond itself. This passage celebrates death's sure defeat, for Christ is raised from the dead. This passage summons the speed-of-light power that overtakes death's darkness. The dead stillness explodes with incomparable, creative power that creates a new family, in Christ, that we call the church.

Paul never states why he uses the image of body of Christ to describe the church. But I have a theory. On the road to Damascus, when the bright light shone from heaven and the voice spoke, it asked a single question: Saul, why do you persecute me? (Acts 9:4). Paul was on his way to persecute the followers of Jesus. To the Lord, it was as if Paul/Saul was persecuting Jesus himself. Indeed, Jesus declares that it is *he* whom Paul is persecuting (9:5). Perhaps from this life-altering encounter, Paul saw not only Jesus of Nazareth in a totally new way, but also Jesus's followers as intimately connected to their Lord, the head of the body.

Preaching on *kephalē* is difficult because of the ubiquity of the term "headship" as a principle of authority and (hierarchical) order in the English language and church culture. Lee-Barnewall captures an essential aspect of

Paul's metaphor, namely its mysterious revelation of God's love that shows no favoritism. The head, Christ, uses his preeminence to save his body, the church. Paul says it so well in Phil 2:6–8, that Jesus took on a human body, and died a horrific human death, that he might redeem humanity.

Preaching on the church can be equally difficult. What the church is not, in Paul's mind, is a building. Too often church boards protect the establishment or focus primarily on financial growth to support building needs. For Paul, the church is *people*. Especially today with many people eschewing formal worship in buildings, this message—the church is people—needs to be lived out. People of all ages are staying away from buildings yet are interested in community. Churches that develop service opportunities and challenge believers to love as Christ does, offer an antidote to the malaise that affects so many in the West.

The church operates at both the local and the universal level. Each local body is to be unified, and each local group is to think of other churches' needs. We see this in Paul's collection for the believers in Judea, which he promoted in his primarily gentile churches. He asked that each local church put aside money that could be collected and taken to those Judean churches that were struggling (see 2 Cor 8–9). In Ephesians, Paul attends to the universal church in 2:6 and 5:5, and the local community in 4:25, 32. The universal nature of the church is not limited by time, which means that the earliest believers in Ephesus are in some real sense also members of our churches today. Some churches in the West celebrate that reality by remembering on November 2nd, All Souls' Day, the former church members who have died in Christ.[19] Families are encouraged to send in a photo of their loved ones to honor them in the congregation.

Praying together as a congregation is one of the privileges believers have. Praying the prayers written in Scripture can open new avenues for believers to relate to each other and to God. I am often struck with how different my prayers are from those Paul prays in Ephesians. I tend to focus on immediate circumstances and health issues. I try to remember to confess my sins and to offer praise for who God is. But in comparison to Paul's prayers, mine are small. Paul's prayers are theologically rich, mine are materially poor. Paul's prayers are filled with worship, mine can feel transactional. Paul prays that his fellow believers know God more deeply and know their own worth in God's eyes. Paul's prayer here focuses not

---

19. All Saints Day, November 1, celebrates the saints and martyrs of the church. Eastern Orthodox churches celebrate All Saints Day the first Sunday after Pentecost.

only on what is going on now, but what is yet to come. We enjoy benefits of being a member of God's family, adopted through Christ. And we await full benefits in our resurrected state. Paul's prayer points us to eternity. From that perspective, we can, like Paul, start and end with thanksgiving.

EPHESIANS 2

Ephesians 2:1–10: "By Grace You Have Been Saved"

THE SECOND CHAPTER TAKES a fearless look at the realities of sin and evil that impact and influence human reality. In chapter 1, Paul presented a magnificent picture of God's salvation plan, including exalted language regarding God's power that raised Christ from the dead. God seated Christ in the place of supreme honor at his side. Paul rejoices that God established the church as Christ's body, full of the fullness of God, loved beyond measure (1:22–23). Following the exalted picture of Christ raised above all names, having all enemies under his feet, and establishing his church, Paul tells the story of opposites, reveals the character of God, and holds a mirror to the self. The story sweeps across our past, our present, into our future, and attends to both the world around us, and the spiritual activities taking place at the same time. Paul turns his gaze to the human plight around him. Paul sees two groups of humans, Jews and gentiles, divided based on God's election of Israel as heir of the covenants and promises. The groups share in their human frailty, but only the Jew has God's self-revelation and law by which to know the one true God. The gentiles, pagan in their religious understanding, stand far from God and under the control or sway of the evil spiritual forces that draw humans away from God's goodness and holiness (2:1–2). Paul looks at the human plight and its redemption from two different angles in this chapter. First, Paul focuses on the spiritual realities that exist in the heavenly places, both the ruler of the earthly kingdoms and Christ and his followers, who are seated with him above at God's throne (2:5–6). Second, Paul addresses the social realities faced by gentiles who experienced life outside of God's community, Israel (2:12). Paul emphasizes the new community created by Christ's death on the cross, bringing Jew and gentile into a single worshipping community, a new family created by

God through Christ, with the Holy Spirit enabling unity with God and each other.

Looking at the first ten verses (2:1–10), we find human sin and frailty exposed, but salvation promised in the one who conquered death. In a sentence that spans the first seven verses, Paul identifies the pitiful situation of humanity, Jew and gentile, in this present evil age, and the great kindness of God to deliver through his grace in Christ. Paul finishes this section with two relatively short sentences that emphasize God's gift of grace and his ongoing work in believers' lives.

Paul lays out a narrative in these ten verses that creates the framework for his theological claims. He sketches the reality of the gentile, a person who has been led around by a spiritual force that controls this age and draws people from God. Nevertheless, Paul laments that "we" Jews struggle, not by living into the sin, but by falling prey to our weak flesh that desires unholy things. This bleak narrative does not end here, fortunately. Paul introduces God and his salvation plan. Paul extols God's gift of new life in Christ. He declares that God's grace has saved them. The gift of grace is received by faith and is given without regard to the person's worth. The end is not, however, to merely rescue believers from their lives of sin and passions but to set them on a path of good works. Said another way, while believers do enjoy a seat next to Christ in the heavenlies, they also have good works to do in their daily routines. The purposes of salvation are two-fold: to bring believers into relationship with God through Christ and to further God's work in this world by doing the good works God has arranged for believers to do.

The narrative underpinning these ten verses is built on a string of opposites and ostensible contradictions that reinforce God's great love for us. The opposites fall into several categories. First, there is the temporal/eternal pairing, which maps onto the reality that this current age is ruled by the ruler of the "air" that foments disobedience, and yet God's work in Christ has broken that ruler's ultimate power. Believers have a foot in each world, as they are now raised and seated with Christ and are called to do good works in this present age of sinfulness. This tension has been described as "already, not yet." Because Christ is raised and because believers are in Christ, therefore believers enjoy eternal life in him. Yet because believers live in a mortal body, they feel the pressure of constant bombardment by sin and their fleshly passions. The hope of the imperishable, immortal body in resurrection remains for now a hope. But it is a sure hope because believers already have Christ's life in them (see also Rom 8:34–39; Gal 2:20).

Second, we have the opposites that characterize the believer. Paul recognizes the differences between the gentile alienation from God, a predicament that he elaborates upon in the second half of the chapter, and the Jew, who knows and loves the God of creation. The Jew can take comfort in knowing God's mercy, but as Paul felt himself, there would also be frustration in the weakness of his human nature that drove him to follow his passions. Paul explains this well in Rom 7:14–25, which is a parallel passage to Eph 2:3. In Romans, Paul describes the dilemma he and other Jews experienced.

They rejoice in God's law, for it is holy and reveals the true God's love for all people, and especially his mercy to the faithful. But Paul also despaired because the law would not empower him against his weak flesh, and he ended up succumbing to its desires, in disobedience to the very law he loves. Both in Romans, and here in Ephesians, Paul concludes on a note of rejoicing, for God does not leave him (or any other person) as a prisoner to their own weak flesh, but grants freedom in new life in Christ. Let me state clearly: Rom 7 is not about the Christian life, but about the life of a Jew who delights in God's law but is unable to fulfill it, because the law itself has no power to overcome the power of sin and the ruler of this world. Only in Christ is a person free because the Holy Spirit gives new life (Rom 8:1–3). The Christian life is one freed from slavery to sin (Rom 6:17–18). To claim, as some Christians do, that Rom 7 is about the Christian life is to misread Rom 6 and 8 and to fail to fully accept the new-creature status that is each believer's in Christ. That said, it is the case that believers still struggle against sin, but they are able, in Christ, to resist its power, for they are no longer its slaves.

Third, there is a powerful contrast between the loving God and the ruler of the powers of the air. The latter leads people into sin, which causes God's righteous judgment to fall on them. The sins committed include all manner of domination over others and abuse and greed. The focus on satisfying the self becomes malignant and eats at relationships and scars families. Sin hurts and is hurtful. Sin's effects spiral out to others and to God's creation. Contrast the grasping, deceitful god of this age with the super-abundant mercy of God, whose love is so powerful as to defeat death and to make alive those who have no loveliness in them. This God makes alive, raises up, gives a seat of honor, and gives purpose to life now by making ready good works that believers can do.

Ephesians 2:1–3

The first three verses (2:1–3) explain the dire straits experienced by the characters of this salvation story. Paul begins with "you" in 2:1, and the question arises whether this "you" is simply anyone before they receive Christ or is a gentile pagan. The former case is based on the lack of specificity here, in contrast to Paul's direct mention of the gentile pagan status in 2:11. And the assumption is made that Paul's focus is on the individual and his or her personal salvation. However, it is more likely that Paul describes the past experiences of the gentile believers in their paganism. Paul states that they were dead, because of their sins. But the problem is much bigger than an individual's sinful deeds. Paul describes the power that evil spiritual forces have currently over those who do not know God. Paul identifies the ruler of the kingdom or authority of the air as one who sponsors disobedience against God's ways (2:2). Likely these are the same forces that Paul warns against at the end of the epistle when he asks believers to put on the armor of God (6:12). Gentiles living in Ephesus would have revered Artemis of the Ephesians by participating in regular festivals in her honor. They would have supported the imperial cult and the goddess Roma and turned to specific deities for help with illnesses or finances. Paul lists specific sins later in the epistle, such as coveting, obscenity, sexual immorality, and greed (4:17–19; 5:3–6). Paganism led to death, for it supported the ruler of this evil age, this age of disobedience. It is hard to imagine Paul describing his life in Judaism in this way. He speaks similarly to the Colossians, that those gentiles were dead in their sins and the uncircumcision of their flesh until they were made alive in Christ (Col 2:13).

Of course, gentiles in Ephesus would not have described their lives in such terms. They would have offered reverence to their patron deity, Artemis, and desired to give her honor so that she would take care of their city, and its residences, especially at the time of childbirth. They would also have feared the ever-present spiritual forces and sought protection through amulets and magic. They would honor with votive offerings a god or goddess for healing or safe passage on a journey. So too today, people worry about health, about job security, about protection from violence. They might use horoscopes or seek mystical experiences to reduce their fear and loneliness.

This sort of spirituality is unable to defeat the powerful forces that spread fear and encourage sin and brokenness. Fortunately, Paul provides an answer to the world's attempts at wholeness and joy as he describes God's great love and mercy below.

While the gentile was walking after things of this world, things that led one away from God and his goodness, Jews in Ephesus resisted the ruler of this earthly realm. They followed the one true God and desired to serve him. The Jews know the way of godliness and yet find themselves failing to live in the way they know pleases God. Paul laments that his weak flesh led him to indulge in his passions. In this, he was not so much deceived by the prince of the kingdom of the air, but unable to stand firm against such temptation. Both Jew and gentile fall under God's just condemnation because all have sinned. Why, then, does it matter that we distinguish Jew and gentile in these three verses? Aside from being more historically accurate to Paul's time, it is important to notice the incredible power held by the prince of the kingdom of the air. Knowledge of God's ways does not protect from the spirit who promotes disobedience, then or now.

In the end, Paul declares that both Jew and gentile, having taken separate paths, find themselves at the same dead end. Paul says that all are "by nature" children under God's judgment of sin. The phrase "by nature" (*physis*) often refers to a person's birth. It may be that Paul is contrasting humanity's natural state, with believers' adoption into God's family through Christ. Paul speaks of being under God's wrath or anger (*orgē*). Human anger is often expressed with out-of-control violence, seeking revenge and destruction. God's wrath is far from this, for his wrath is linked with his righteous justice that he establishes in his good and gracious kingdom. The prophet Isaiah speaks of God's wrath in the context of Israel. He explains that though Israel sinned, God will rescue even as he rejects their disobedience. God's wrath brings destruction on those who oppress but gives time for repentance (Isa 30:27–28; 59:2–13; 63:3–4). We desire that God's wrath be executed against those who have sinned against us or harmed us, yet we desire mercy when we have sinned against others or caused harm. Paul assures us that God in Christ hears our cry for forgiveness and turns away his wrath.

Ephesians 2:4–7

Notice the sharp contrast between this verse and the previous one. The narrative tension of the last three verses of gloom and doom is relieved in verse 4 as Paul extols God's gift of new life in Christ. Paul declares that God is rich in mercy and loves us with a great love. In the Greek, Paul uses both the noun (*agape*) and the verb "to love" (*agapeō*) as he emphasizes the limitless love that underpins God's salvation plan. Paul declares that God rescues all people, because all people are dead in their sins, and God brings new life in Christ. God's actions relate back to his actions in Christ. In chapter 1, we learn that God raised Christ and seated him at his right hand (1:20). God put his enemies at his feet and made him head over all things.

Death due to sins has been overturned by granting new life in Christ. This new life has important characteristics. First, it occurs "in" or "with" Christ, as Paul adds a prefix to the verbs that signal a joining together of the believer and Christ. Second, this implies that salvation is not (only) a status or static category, but a living relationship between God and the believer. Third, this relationship overcomes material or earthly constraints, as the believer is seated with Christ in the heavenlies. The believer is removed from the sphere dominated by the disobedient into a space of unencumbered life, a place of honor at Christ's side.

Probably sensing that such riches would be hard for the readers and listeners to grasp, Paul continues to describe this new life in Christ. This grace is based on the love of God with which he loved—Paul uses both the noun and the verb in 2:4 to reinforce his point. The grace reflects God's kindness, his mercy, all available in abundance beyond our imagination. The new life in Christ is designed to equip believers for good works that have already be laid out by God.

The lengthy sentence that spans 2:1–7 has as its subject God (2:4) and three verbs: to make alive, to raise up, and to seat. Before looking at the verbs, we should attend to the description of God. Paul indicates that God is rich in mercy, an idea he repeats several times in this epistle (1:7, 18; 2:7; 3:16). God's riches can be seen in his grace, his inheritance that he gives to his people; Christ also possesses infinite riches (3:8). God's mercy and love are boundless. The Greek term for mercy, *eleos*, is often used to translate the Hebrew term that describes God's steadfast love, *hesed*. For example, the Lord revealed himself to Moses on Mount Sinai as the one who is compassionate, gracious, "slow to anger, *abounding in love* and faithfulness, maintaining *love* to thousands and forgiving wickedness, rebellion, and sin" (Exod 34:6–7 NIV 2011; italics convey *hesed*).

Paul emphasizes three acts done by God, and each one is accomplished with Christ. All three actions relate to his actions in raising Christ and seating him at his right hand (1:20). Each of these three verbs is in the aorist tense, which is unusual for Paul. The aorist tense tends to either focus on a past event, or present a perfective or external, summary view of the action.[1] If one assumes that the aorist indicates *only* events that occurred in the past, this might create confusion in the reader because, typically, Paul speaks of believers' salvation as a future event, to be enjoyed in the final day (Rom 5:9–10), or perhaps in some way occurring now (2 Cor 6:2). However, because aorist is also used to describe an event from a wide-angle lens, from an outsider's viewpoint, or from a bird's eye view, without regard to when or how long the event was, then the aorist tense here is understandable. After all, God's work in Christ is cosmic in scope, and the aorist captures the panoramic view of God's all-surpassing love.

The passage in Romans offers another point of contrast, as Paul locates believers' redemption in the cross, not the resurrection and ascension of Christ (Rom 5:6–10). Yet this difference is well within Paul's range of theological understanding of God's salvation plan, which emphasizes both the realized and the future aspects of believers' inheritance in Christ. Paul stresses the realized or present victory in Christ here in Ephesians, but we see it elsewhere in his letters (Rom 8:10; 2 Cor 3:18; Phil 3:20).[2]

First, God made us alive with Christ (2:5; see also Col 2:13). The aorist tense used here and in the other two verbs, could suggest that Paul speaks proleptically, referring to the future resurrection, when believers receive their raised, glorified bodies (Phil 3:20–21). This may be his point to the Colossians, where the focus is cancelation of debts and forgiveness of sins (2:13). However, here Paul is more likely emphasizing the current status of Christ's victory, for several reasons. First, as noted above, the aorist tense here is constative, it emphasizes the entire work of salvation, the cross, resurrection, and ascension of Christ, and by extension, believers in Christ. Second, Paul emphasizes Christ's victory over spiritual forces both at the beginning of this chapter and the end of the previous one. Third, Jesus Christ's resurrection and ascension affect believers now as evidence

---

1. For a discussion of Greek verbs, see Campbell, *Basics of Verbal Aspect in Biblical Greek*.

2. Thielman, *Ephesians*, 135–37.

of their redemption and forgiveness of sins. Fourth, Paul stresses the power and wisdom of God's work in Christ, this mystery of salvation, is now on display before the spiritual beings and forces (3:10).

Between the first and second verbs, Paul bursts forth: "by grace you have been saved" (2:5, 8). The perfect passive participle can also be rendered, "you are saved," because the tense signals a past event that continues to affect the present. The passive voice emphasizes that it is God who acts. The outburst here in 2:5 will be picked up in 2:8, with additional details and depth. Suffice it to say here that the gift of grace is received by faith and is given without regard to the person's worth. The end is not, however, to merely rescue believers from their lives of sin and passions, but to set them on a path of good works.

Paul continues that God has raised us with Christ and seated us with Christ (2:6). Paul stresses that believers are "in Christ," participate in his life eternal. Paul declared that he has been crucified with Christ, that now Christ lives in him (Gal 2:20). If he is in Christ, then he is where Christ is. Paul plays out this logic and concludes that believers share now in the life of Christ, who is in the heavenlies with the Father. Recall in the first chapter, Paul emphasizes that Christ died and was raised and is seated with God at his right hand (1:20–21). So too here, Paul points out that humans are dead in their sins and experience new life in Christ in the heavenlies (1:20; 2:6). The heavenly places represent the realm of God, with the lesser "gods" existing in the atmosphere or air and humans living on earth, being greatly impacted by the other realms.

In 2:7, Paul reiterates God's grace in Christ in three specific ways. First, he points to the impact it has across time. God's grace extends beyond the horizon, having begun with the incarnation (Gal 4:4–5) and extended to the ascension and to Christ's second coming (Phil 3:20–21) and continuing throughout the new heavens and new earth, the kingdom of Christ and of God (Eph 5:5). Second, he describes this grace as having immeasurable riches. In 2:4, Paul spoke of God's rich mercy, and in the previous chapter he declared the riches of God's grace (1:7). Here we have the phrase repeated, with the addition of the word "immeasurable" to capture the extent of God's beautiful salvation plan. Third, Paul states that God's grace reveals God's kindness. Too often, God's grace takes on an abstract quality, a doctrinal distance. Paul reminds us that God's kindness is at work in establishing believers' adoption. Today, to say someone is kind often means only that they are polite. But for Paul, kindness carries a sense of generosity, compassion, and moral excellence.

Ephesians 2:8–10

These three verses offer a summary of God's salvation gift, which reveals his grace. Key terms include grace and faith, which we have seen already, and works and good works, which Paul develops along with the noun "gift." We know that God's grace expresses his mercy, his kindness, his power, his riches, and his love. We heard of "faith" in 1:15, as Paul praised the Ephesians for their faith in the Lord Jesus and their love of all believers (saints). In this passage, Paul juxtaposes faith and works, and works and "good works," a phrase we do not see outside of Ephesians (similar phrase found in 2 Cor 9:8; Col 1:10; 1 Thess 1:3). Paul introduces the term "gift" (he uses a related Greek term in 3:7 and 4:7). Each of these terms will be examined below as we walk through these verses.

In 2:8, Paul repeats the phrase "by grace you have been saved" (see also 2:5). Here he adds "by faith." The noun "faith" (*pistis*) includes a range of meanings: loyalty, faithfulness, assurance, and body of belief.[3] Paul uses the noun several times in Ephesians, sometimes in reference to the believers' confidence in the gospel message of salvation in Christ (1:15; 3:17; 4:5, 13). There are a few places, including here in 2:8, where questions arise as to whether this grammatical construction ("through faith," preposition and noun in the genitive case) is an objective genitive (faith in Christ) or subjective genitive (Christ's own faithfulness).[4] In Eph 3:12, we read a similar phrase, with the addition of the genitive pronoun referring to Christ. Paul speaks here about the boldness and confidence believers have in praying to God, based on the salvation plan that is accomplished in Christ. We could translate the phrase "through faith in Christ" (objective genitive) or "through Christ's faithfulness" (subjective genitive).[5] In 2:8, readers must decide if Paul stresses Christ's faithfulness, in which case he links "riches"

---

3. Matlock, "Detheologizing the ΠΙΣΤΙΣ ΧΡΙΣΤΟΥ Debate," 1–23.

4. διὰ πίστεως Ἰησοῦ Χριστοῦ (Rom 3:22; Gal 2:16), διὰ πίστεως Χριστοῦ (Phil 3:9), ἐκ πίστεως Χριστοῦ (Rom 3:26; Gal 2:16), ἐκ πίστεως Ἰησου Χριστοῦ (Gal 3:22), ἐν πίστει (Gal 2:20). In all of these verses, the context also speaks about the δικαιοσύνη θεου (righteousness of God).

5. For a discussion on these verses, see Foster, "Πιστις Χριστου Terminology in Philippians and Ephesians," 99–109. See also Bell, "Faith in Christ," 111–25.

in 2:7 and "gift" in 2:9 with Christ's role in God's grace displayed in the salvation plan. In this case, Paul would be drawing attention to a contrast between Christ's faithfulness and any sort of faithfulness a believer might exhibit ("not of yourselves"). Alternatively, Paul could be focused on believers' faith in the grace of God, as in 1:13, in which case the phrase is an objective genitive. Grammar rules alone will not settle the matter; theological claims about the nature of God's gift, as well as the meaning of "works," often play a role in deciding how to interpret the enigmatic phrase. For some, the objective genitive highlights the believer's lack of any involvement in earning salvation, for it is a "free" gift. For others, the subjective genitive spotlights the work of Christ and believers' place as being in Christ.

Paul connects "of yourselves" (2:8) and "of works" (2:9) to conclude that no one can rightfully boast. What does Paul intend with the phrase "by works"? Often this is read as referring to the Old Testament law, perhaps to Jews seeking to gain merit and do works to gain their salvation. In the aftermath of the Holocaust, New Testament research has shown new insights into Judaism in Paul's day, including that Jews stressed their election by God, and so did not try to earn merit for salvation.[6] Others point to human efforts broadly through careful conduct and pious acts. We might gain clarity by looking at Paul's fear, namely that someone's works might lead to boasting.

What might the Ephesians boast in? Is it their pride in seeking to achieve salvation on their own terms or by impressing God with their own deeds? What would a gentile pagan, the typical past of an Ephesian believer, be tempted to boast about before God? Certainly not doing God's law. Probably they would be tempted to rest on their social worth, their sense that God chose them because of an inherent good quality that they possessed. The Roman world was highly stratified, and social honor was a prized possession. But God shows no favoritism (6:9). No one can boast that they have within them some special worth that God saw and so chose them. Nor did God act on some foreknowledge that the person would turn out to be worthy. Paul is clear that the social-worth game played in society has no influence upon God. His abundant grace is available to all; it is for everyone, and it is received through faith in Christ.

Boasting in the ancient world did not always carry the negative assumptions of self-promotion that its modern use does. In Paul's day, boasting was acceptable if it was true, if it spoke rightly about the worth of an

---

6. For a brief overview, see Yinger, "Interpretation," 516–21.

object or person. In its best form, boasting gave honor to whom it was due. Jeremiah's call to let the one who boasts boast in the Lord was shared by Paul (1 Cor 1:31; 2 Cor 10:17). Paul informs the Galatians that believers could boast in their actions if they spoke of them truthfully and if they were not making a comparison with another believer (Gal 6:4).

When we take boasting into account and reflect on the meaning of gift and grace in the ancient world, it is likely that Paul intends in 2:9 to warn believers against dishonoring God. They could dishonor God and his gift of grace in at least two ways. On the one hand, they might doubt that God's gift could truly be for them, as their social worth was so low. Paul's teaching would have resonated with the slaves and freed-persons in the congregation, those who would have no reason for pride in anything they might achieve. Slaves were on the bottom rung of the social ladder and bore social shame. They could hardly have believed that God would give them such an over-abundant gift, an inheritance in Christ. Paul comforts them that the (false) evaluation by society of their lack of social/ethnic/wealth status is of no importance to God. On the other hand, the Ephesians could dishonor God if they assumed that their social worth attracted God so that he gave them his gift of grace. A few in the congregation might have higher social worth or felt an ethnic pride and would perhaps imagine that God proved himself wise in choosing them. For them, this verse reminded them that God is no respecter of persons; he shows no favoritism (6:9). Thinking of works and boasting in relationship to social worth helps us grasp a key aspect of God's gift of grace.

It is another evidence of God's grace that believers are his handiwork, in Christ empowered for good works (1:10; Phil 2:12–13). Paul calls to mind the creation itself, as he uses the noun only one other time—when he speaks of God creating the cosmos (Rom 1:20). The cognate verb is used to describe God's work with clay vessels (Isa 29:16, cited in Rom 9:20). God graciously gives purpose to his family members, who can bring honor to their Father. These good works will further develop their holiness, for believers were created to be holy and blameless (1:4). These good works reflect the God's character and will provide opportunities for believers to show God's love, kindness, love, and mercy in the church and the wider world and thus bring honor and praise to God.

Ephesians 2:1–10: Reflections for Preaching and Teaching

We might call this section a cultural "lost and found," for humans live in a lost world, one that wandered from God's ways to follow the ways of evil, shameful deeds and passions. From this lost state, we discover we are found in Christ because God's rich grace pursues us. Sometimes we need to be reminded just how lost our world is because we grow accustomed to its "me first" priorities and the arrogance and shame that follows. We get used to the injustice, the power-plays, and the trauma that follows. The lost can't fix their lost state, but they have already been found by God, who through Christ offers a way out of worldly patterns of life.

We could also think of this passage as "Healthcare 101." We live in a contaminated world, polluted with sin that clogs our arteries, stains our lungs, and weighs us down with terminal diagnoses. God, the great Healer, cures believers through Christ, mending and repairing them so they can live holy, fruitful lives. The "so that" in the previous sentence must be stressed. Even as physicians do not simply want to cure a disease but bring a person back to a flourishing life, so too God's grace is not meant only to redeem from sin, but to give the believer the opportunity to live a new life (Rom 6:4). God's redemption is of the total self, body and soul, enfolded completely in God's kindness, creating believers as living examples of God's gift of grace that speaks against the polluting power of the rulers of this age.

The Ephesians would have expected that God gave the gift expecting a response: namely, that the believer would express thanksgiving and worship. I think Paul would agree that this response was a worthy one, and even more, that believers would embrace the new relationship they have in Christ. Today around the world, believers lift their voices in praise to the God of their salvation. This part of Paul's teaching is clear, if not always easy to live into.

But in another way, this gift from God shook up conventional wisdom about gift-giving. Both in Paul's day, and today, gifts are given to those who deserve them, who show promise or are worthy in some way, in other words, they are based on works. The "no strings attached" gift valued in modern western culture is not the ideal in the ancient world, nor is it Paul's understanding. God's magnanimous gift of grace creates a relationship with those who accept it.

What does this relationship look like? It includes doing good works. Stay with me here! There are two types of "works" discussed in Ephesians 2:8–10, and we should distinguish both of these "works" from another phrase of Paul's, "works of the law." This latter phrase is used in Rom 3 and has to do with specific laws, such as circumcision, that represent the Jewish path of holy living with which Paul was familiar. Such a pathway of following the law is not in itself bad or inherently self-focused, but now in Christ, both Jew and gentile are guided by the Holy Spirit on the pathway of holy living.

Paul indicates that God created "good works" for us to do. Doing "good works" has nothing to do with "earning" salvation; rather, the Ephesians would be demonstrating their redeemed life in Christ by doing the works prepared by the one whom they desire to honor. These good works could be specific to an individual. For example, Paul explains to the Corinthians that he worked harder than the other apostles, yet it was the grace of God working in him (1 Cor 15:8; see also Col 4:17). The good works might also be general deeds of virtue as outlined in the last three chapters of our epistle.

Paul describes the believer as God's *poiēma*, his special work or his special creation. In the end, it is *God's* work that matters, not our works. Do we really live into the beauty of this astonishing truth? In many churches today, success is equated with faithfulness. The worth of our efforts is measured by the size or efficiency of a program or budget. There is a drive to prove oneself worthy of God's gift. There is fear that God will realize what a bad choice he made in giving his gift of grace to a sinner like me. And there is a judgmental mindset that looks at other believers, and questions God's wisdom in extending the gift of grace to them. In these ways we repeat the struggles of the Ephesians, who were busy grading themselves and others, rather than walking in the truth that each believer represents God's handiwork.

Ephesians 2:11–23: Christ Is Our Peace

Paul reminds us we are on a journey. In this passage, people move from far away to closer in. They move from outside the house, to inside. They move their status from outsiders and foreigners to family members within the home. This journey was also from despair to joy, from then to now. It moved from a pointless existence of godlessness to a life of good works laid before the person empowered to accomplish them (2:10). Paul declared in the opening lines of his letter that God established a salvation plan that would unite us with Christ to be holy and blameless. The goal is more than saving our souls or forgiving our sins. It is to be holy and blameless; a life lived that honors God. Paul restates this truth in 2:10, that, in Christ, we are purposed or created to do good works, that is, those deeds that demonstrate God's holiness, justice, mercy, and joy in the world.

When Paul begins our passage with "therefore," he draws on the conviction that God has made us in Christ to live out our union with Christ through activities that he has prepared for us. Paul builds on the truth that believers, both Jew and gentile, are God's handiwork, his creation. Paul asks that gentiles remember their past so that they can better imagine their future. Their journey from paganism to faith in Christ is described in spatial, social, and religious categories.

First, Paul uses spatial terms, near and far, as he paints a picture of the gentile coming to God. Paul did not create this image, for he draws on Isaiah's vision that God will gather those far and near, in peace and healing (Isa 57:19). In Paul's day, many people took pilgrimages to holy sites, and this would be especially true in Ephesus, where thousands would travel to see the great temple of Artemis. Festivals would process through the main streets to her temple a few kilometers outside the city center. Many were "brought near" to the great goddess herself, whose a colossus statue would represent her presence. Paul wants believers to reimagine the journey, now to a new temple, to worship the one true God. Jewish believers share the road with gentile believers, both living in Christ.

Second, Paul uses religious categories of Jew and pagan as he describes the new creation that brings together this most unlikely pair. Paul speaks of the gentile pagan's separation from God's promises, the covenants that God made with his people, and thus the hope and joy that comes with knowing the one true God. Slipped amid this dismal description of the gentile pagan's life is a comment about those who circumcise. Paul notes that there are those who label a gentile as "uncircumcised." This is at one level simply stating a fact. However, the comment is mainly intended as condemnation, for circumcision was shorthand for a life pursuing holiness, a life among the people of God. Yet Paul does not support those who call themselves the circumcision, even though he was once one of them. Now he considers the greatness of life in Christ, with the empowering Holy Spirit, as the way to achieve his lifelong ambition—a holy life (see also Phil 3:7–8).

Third, Paul uses social categories, and emphasizes opposites, including having citizenship or not, being in your own home, or a foreigner. He speaks of citizenship and the lack thereof. The Greek term *politeia* has a broader meaning than what we typically think about citizenship today. The word included the sense of a way of life and conduct that demarcated one group from others. Jews living in cities around the Roman Empire would form a social group that could be called a commonwealth, and Paul uses this term to speak of believers' citizenship being in heaven (Phil 3:20, *políteuma*). Paul reminds the Ephesian gentile believers that they are now fellow citizens with Jewish believers in Christ and thus members of God's family.

Another social category is that of family, and Paul describes believers as members of a single family in Christ, all receiving the Holy Spirit. The gentile believer is now sharing the house of God with Jewish followers of Jesus. This household image reflects Paul's earlier insistence that God adopted believers through the work of his Son (Eph 1:5). Each household has their own way of doing things, and in God's family, each believer is co-heir with Christ who shares in all the promises of God (3:6).

This gospel reality is easier to say than do, and much of Paul's ministry to the Romans and Corinthians is trying to help the community of Jewish and gentile believers do life together. Problems arose around whether to keep certain Jewish practices (rest on Sabbath, kosher food habits) and what gentile practices could be continued (eating meat sacrificed to idols). The struggle sometimes came to a head, as it did in Antioch with the apostle Peter when Peter withdrew from eating with gentile believers after having previously done so (Gal 2:11–13). For any church, it is of supreme importance that it regularly examines what about its culture is harmless, what is beneficial, and what is dangerous to gospel living. Paul's measuring stick is the practice's adherence to the gospel message. For example, Paul critiques the Corinthians for desiring a public persona that meets their culture's social criteria of wisdom and celebrity, but Paul counters that such criteria will empty the cross of its power (I continue to be astounded that a preacher's ego or educational prowess can eviscerate the power that brings the dead to life.). Again, Paul asks the Romans not to divide over what they can and cannot eat, but rather to focus on righteousness, peace, and joy in the Holy Spirit (Rom 14:17).

A final social category is that of friend and enemy. Paul knew of and would have personally experienced hostility at times from gentile pagans because he was Jewish. And certainly, violence would go the other way, in places where Jews were the majority. Tensions could be high in Jerusalem, for example, especially during festivals as both groups taunted each other. Into this tension, Christ brings peace.

Ephesians 2:11–13

The first of three sections in the passage describes the plight of the gentile believers in their pagan past (2:11–13). As difficult as it may be, Paul commands them to remember where they were, so as to better appreciate where they are. Paul does not sugarcoat their life before knowing Christ. He identifies the gentile men as uncircumcised (circumcision being a symbol among Jews of inclusion in God's covenant family). Paul does not seek their physical circumcision, for he holds that believers are the "true circumcision" (Phil 3:3), a spiritual circumcision of the heart (Deut 10:16; Jer 4:4). Paul continues with language that stresses separation, alienation, hopelessness. He declares that they are without God, by which he means that they did not know the one true God but were mired in their paganism.

The picture is not merely of the individual but of a community that lacked the guidance and direction that only God could provide. Community was crucial for self-identity in the ancient world and in many cultures today. The place of most security was within one's community, yet gentile pagans were outside of, and far from, the community of God. Paul speaks about the commonwealth of Israel, Jewish communities in cities around the Roman Empire that worship the one true God. Jews in Ephesus probably met regularly for Sabbath, observed food laws such as not eating pork, and tithed money to the Jerusalem Temple.[7] They benefitted from the covenants and the promise of the messiah, while the gentiles were foreigners to it all. Yet, Paul concludes the gentiles are no longer far if they are in Christ. It is his blood, his crucifixion, which drew gentiles into God's family.

This picture highlights that Jews were not actively proselytizing gentiles; however, from the inscriptions and comments in Roman historians' work, we know that some (a few?) gentiles frequented the synagogue, interested in the Mosaic law and Jewish traditions. These "god-fearers" might become Christians, as Lydia did (Acts 16:14; see also Josephus, *Ag. Ap.* 2.210). Paul does not blame Jews for the plight of the gentiles, for they are not excluding gentiles from hearing God's word (Acts 15:19–21). This is important to notice, because in the next section, Paul speaks of enmity between Jew and gentile being resolved in Christ. The hostility was created by the gentiles who resist God. The tensions were the result of the covenants of God which established standards for holiness and justice. And the answer

---

7. Trebilco, *Early Christians in Ephesus*, 40.

is found in Christ's redeeming death, which brought together those both near and far from God.

Ephesians 2:14–18

The heart of this passage is the declaration that Christ himself is our peace (2:14). The peace has many facets, including salvific and social, and Paul uses metaphors of temple and body to help readers see the dimensions of Christ's work on the cross. Often, we think of the blood of Christ that washes away sin. Very true, but only part of the truth. Here Paul describes the power of Christ's blood to remake human community, to reconcile past enemies, and to destroy the barriers that separate what must become one.

Christ's work on the cross created a new humanity or people (*anthrōpos*), and Paul likely draws on Isaiah's picture of the house of Israel and the people of Judah. Paul develops the metaphor of the body of Christ, which he announced at the end of chapter 1. Christ reconciles the two groups, Jews and gentiles, in one body (2:16). Christ did not bring a peace treaty that included compromises on both sides as both give a little and get a little. God's answer to strife and hostility is to put these enmities to death in Christ. Also put to death was human traditions that served to separate these two groups. It was through Jesus's own death, in his flesh (2:15), that he accomplished this work. With his death on the cross, the law was set aside as the foundation for the people of God, and Christ is established as the cornerstone (2:20).

In setting aside the foundational status of the law, or nullifying it now that Christ has made a new people, Paul does not imagine that he gives up his Jewishness, nor did it nullify his gentile coworkers' gentile-ness (for example, Titus or Syntyche). Paul still attended festivals in Jerusalem, and Titus remained uncircumcised. The new humanity that is Christ's peace assigned less value to Jew and gentile distinctive behaviors and put most emphasis on Christ as the one in whom they live and grow. Each person who becomes part of this new body has died to the social enmity that previously defined them. The believer is now part of a new entity, a new humanity, a new family, and has a new relationship with God the Father by the Holy Spirit.

Christ is our peace, a peace that destroys hostility and creates unity among those who share equally as God's adopted children. The peace of Christ is vastly different from Roman peace, *pax Romana*, in which hostilities were brutally put down, and barriers erected to impose social hierarchies that favored the elite. Rome's idea of creating peace is to crucify any who challenge it—this reality would not be lost on the Ephesians. Recall that the town clerk, when the riot against Paul's teaching was reaching fever pitch, quieted the crowd with a warning that should things get out of control, Rome would be happy to take away their privileges as a free city to govern themselves (Acts 19:40).

Christ is our peace, a peace that reflects the *shalom* of God. This peace is not merely an absence of war, but it creates joy and goodness, it leads to human flourishing. This peace brings reconciliation with others and with God (Col 1:20). The peace also rests within us, allowing us to let go of anxiety and focus on what is true (Phil 4:6–9; Col 3:15). Paul likely draws on the Old Testament emphasis that the messiah will bring peace. Zechariah declares that the king will bring peace to the nations (Zech 9:9–10) and Isaiah rejoices in the Prince of Peace (9:6 [9:5 LXX]).

Ephesians 2:19–22

Ephesians 2:19–22 comprise a single sentence that develop two important metaphors for understanding the church, namely God's family and God's temple. Paul spoke of God the Father in 2:18, and he continues here with six nouns, including "household" and "building," that use the root of the Greek term house (*oikos*). The household is the locus of one's identity, and in God's family, every person is of equal social worth. Those who were foreigners and lacked a commonwealth, a nod to his words above (2:12), are now citizens with God's people. They are part of God's house.

Gods lived in temples at this time, so it is an easy conceptual move for Paul to speak of God's household living in God's house and think of God's temple. In fact, Paul uses temple imagery throughout this entire passage. In 2:14, he likely refers to the barrier in the Jerusalem temple that restricted, on pain of death, any gentile from going too close to the Jewish courts of the temple complex, Paul describes Christ as tearing down such dividing walls. No longer were gentiles in their uncleanness in danger of polluting the holy site, for Christ's blood makes a believer pure and clean. Now the temple of God is built with stones representing both Jew and gentile, now joined to the cornerstone, Christ (2:22). It is not enough that walls are torn down, for that does not automatically make reconciliation. There needs to be a building up, a new edifice that represents the unity of the new humanity, Christ's body.

Christ is the cornerstone of the temple (2:20). Paul draws on Isaiah's image of the Lord laying the sure foundation and chosen cornerstone (Isa 28:16; see also Rom 9:33; 1 Pet 2:4–6). Builders use the cornerstone to create plumb walls as they build, straight and true. In the case of the Lord's temple, it is Christ himself who facilitates the building's growth, so that the Ephesian community would experience their unity as a space where the Father, Son, and Holy Spirit dwell. Paul will later pray that Christ will dwell in their hearts, as the Spirit gives strength from the Father (3:16–17).

Ephesians 2:11–22: Reflections for Preaching and Teaching

If the answer is "peace," what was the question? If the solution is "one new humanity," what was the problem? This passage offers a perspective on God's salvation plan that makes sense only through salvation history as we find in the Old Testament, the story of Israel as God's chosen people, and the promises and covenants extended to them. The big question implied in this passage is: What is God's plan for all humanity, which is currently fractured, frustrated, and at war with itself? The answer is unity in Christ. Unity, not sameness. This is a unity free from social and ethnic hierarchy; a unity rooted in the power of the Holy Spirit; a unity in which individuals are joined to become a holy people because they are members of God's household.

How might this unity have been worked out in the ancient church? We see an example in the Philippian church, with Euodia and Syntyche, two female coworkers of Paul. We do not know if they are Jewish or gentile, but we have a record of at least four Jewish women named Euodia at this time.[8] Syntyche is obviously Greek, and while it is possible for a Jewish family to name their daughter after the goddess of Fate, it seems unlikely. Perhaps she was a god-fearer like Lydia. For the sake of argument, I suggest that we look at these coworkers of Paul as a Jew–gentile situation of disunity.

Paul calls upon Euodia and Syntyche to be of *the same mind*, repeating the phrase used in Phil 2:2. To the Romans, Paul uses this phrase twice to encourage them to think of one another above themselves (12:16) and to

8. Ilan, *Lexicon of Jewish Names in Late Antiquity*, 3:272. Euodia is found four times, making it one of the popular names (same as Joanna) with Miriam at twenty-three [highest], Sarah at nineteen, and Salome at fourteen.

live in one mind (in harmony) with each other (15:5; see also 2 Cor 13:11). One need only read 1 Cor 1:11—3:23 to understand how vital church unity is to Paul. Clearly, we cannot overemphasize Paul's conviction concerning the unity of the local church body, that in Christ, believers think with a renewed, transformed mindset that privileges others above themselves.

While some argue that Euodia and Syntyche's problem is minor, unimportant, or incidental, most recent commentators argue that the concern for unity between these believers is central to the letter, if not the primary reason for sending it. Perhaps their situation is representative of the general disunity rampant among the Philippians.[9] Carolyn Osiek[10] and Gordon Fee[11] argue that Paul has been building up to this culmination of his argument for unity made from the beginning of his letter. Paul's unprecedented mention of their names suggests a high degree of concern.

It may be that the church in Philippi met in several houses, much as it did in Corinth. If so, perhaps these women led their respective house churches. We hear of Nympha (Col 4:15), Lydia (Acts 16:15, 40), and Priscilla and Aquila (Rom 16:3–5) having churches meet in their homes. In the first century, the social system of patronage was quite strong, and Paul drew on that when he stayed with Lydia on his first visit to Philippi.

While patrons often held great informal power within a community, and it is possible that Euodia and Syntyche were patrons of Paul or of the Philippian church, some commentators go further to suggest that these women were (also) part of the group of *episkopoi* (bishops) and *diakonoi* (deacons) mentioned by Paul in Phil 1:1. Philippians is the only letter wherein Paul notes these groups specifically in his greetings. The two unusual features—noting these groups in the greeting and mentioning these women by name—could indicate that the women belong in one of these categories.

While we can speculate as to whether Euodia and Syntyche were overseers or deacons, Paul states specifically that they are his co-workers who have worked alongside him in the work of the gospel. Most commentators rightly suggest that the two women disagreed with each other and not that they were together in their opposition to Paul. What might these differences be? Some suggest a theological dispute, but it seems odd that Paul

9. Thurston and Ryan, *Philippians and Philemon*, 142; Peterlin, *Paul's Letter to the Philippians*, 387.

10. Osiek, *Philippians, Philemon*, 109.

11. Fee, *Letter to the Philippians*, 385–86.

would not instruct them further on how to resolve it or provided the correct doctrine. Paul does not take sides in this dispute but asks that the situation be mediated locally. This is a far cry from Paul's insistence on judging the man with his father's wife in 1 Cor 5, a situation of acute theological failure.

Most likely, Euodia and Syntyche disagreed on practice, on how to live out their faith in Christ. Several possibilities present themselves. First, it may be that they struggled with how to accommodate their social class or rank with their Christian walk. In the ancient world, friendship as a social category was *agonistic*, that is, highly competitive. The political and social structures of this time encouraged people to outdo each other. Second, perhaps these women are in a court battle. Peterlin postulates that we might have here a situation similar to that found in 1 Cor 6:1–11 wherein believers were taking each other to court.[12] In favor of this view is that Paul calls for a mediator, much as he does in the Corinthian situation. Third, perhaps these women disputed over administering social aid to the poor in their midst. If they were patrons, and deacons, they would likely have been responsible for aid to the destitute in their midst. In Acts 6:1–6, a problem arose in the church about food distribution to Greek-speaking widows. It is possible that a similar situation arose in Philippi, perhaps between two house churches led by Euodia and Syntyche.

Let me suggest a fourth. Perhaps the issue is a Jew–gentile divide, a failure to live into the "one new humanity" brought by Christ (Eph 2:15). If so, the stress might have been at the point of meals and social gatherings. I'm wondering if their gentile and Jewish backgrounds led them to imagine holiness differently: Did Euodia stress the value of Sabbath, while Syntyche shrugged about its importance? Did Euodia insist that church gatherings are meat-free, and Syntyche chose to make this an issue by bringing ham and cheese sandwiches? In other words, what if we read this issue through the lens of Eph 2 (see also Rom 14–15), the struggle of Jewish and gentile believers trying to worship well together, based on vastly different worship experiences?

The key is that unity matters to Paul because it matters to Christ. Christ made the two into one new humanity, and believers are to *act* like this. The actions of unity show the world how the impossible is possible with God. I think of Cornelius's salvation as described in Acts. Peter presents the gospel of the good news of peace through Christ Jesus to this gentile and his household. Peter was well into his sermon when Holy Spirit interrupts,

12. Peterlin, *Paul's Letter to the Philippians*, 127.

and the gift of the Holy Spirit is poured out on the gentile listeners (Acts 10:44–46). None of the Jewish believers expected this, for why would the *Holy* Spirit come upon an *unholy* idolater. But it happened, they heard God being praised. In other words—the proof of Cornelius's conversion was the irrefutable presence of the Holy Spirit in him (and those gentiles with him). As Peter would later declare, "If God gave them the same gift he gave us [Jews] who believed in the Lord Jesus Christ, who was I to think that I could stand in God's way?" (Acts 11:17 NIV 2011).

Actions speak louder than words, sometimes. The impossible unity of Jew and gentile can happen only by the power of the Holy Spirit, can happen only to those who are part of Christ's body, made as one new humanity. For Euodia and Syntyche, having the same mind evidenced having the mind of Christ, living into the sure promise that they will be transformed into the likeness of his glorious body (3:21). No matter how effective each woman's ministry might have been, their lack of unity greatly distressed Paul because unity models Christ. We do not know whether they resolved their disagreement, but Paul certainly believed it was possible in the power of the Lord.

Why is this unity so difficult to find within churches today? I offer three possibilities for the anxiety around unity. First, we might fear losing our distinctiveness in a vast sea of sameness. Yet unity is not the same as sameness; in fact, unity requires difference, which can serve as markers for the overarching oneness. Second, unity can be viewed as compromising core beliefs. While Paul desires that believers mature in faith and understanding (4:15), he allows a wide latitude for practices and opinions (Rom 14:1—15:13; 1 Cor 9:19–23; Gal 4:12). Recall that within a generation, the church at Ephesus is warned that they have lost their first love, even though they retained right doctrines (Rev 2:1–7). Too often today, political views take the priority over the gospel unity that Christ bought with his blood. Third, unity is relegated to secondary importance because we fail to see that this unity is a direct result of the cross, just as is our forgiveness of sins. Unity is not optional nor a side effect of redemption. It is at the center of what salvation looks like: adopted, forgiven children of God.

EPHESIANS 3

Ephesians 3:1–13:
Paul's Defense of Himself and the Gospel Message

WHERE THERE'S SMOKE, THERE'S fire. This aphorism is often used by gossips who assume some rumor is the smoke that proves the deed, the fire. In this case, the smoke is Paul's chains, his imprisonment, a situation that might suggest he is abandoned by God or at least being chastened. To answer the implicit questions and set the record straight, Paul explains his gospel and his circumstances in light of God's mystery, now revealed. The main points of this section include Paul's defense of his ministry as he sits in Roman custody and a further explanation of his gospel by reinforcing God's actions in establishing and revealing such an astonishing salvation. The first seven verses focus on the gospel message, especially the impact on gentiles becoming coheirs with Jews in Christ. The second half of the section turns attention to the spiritual forces and powers that populate the cosmos and the mystery of the gospel's impact in that realm.

Before proceeding further, we must note that incarceration today, especially in the United States, is a vastly different system than that which existed in Paul's day. And we must be honest that the US systems and institutions are fraught with racism, classism, and sexism. Those convicted of crimes often battle the shame of prison time and have numerous high hurdles to overcome when they are released from prison. We will say more below about how the church can be faithful to those in prison (which include believers and non-believers) and those released from prison.

We are so used to Paul's status as a prisoner that we forget how difficult it was for him. While Paul does not tell us where he was imprisoned as he writes this letter, I take the position that Paul is writing from Rome (Acts 28:30–31). Paul was not convicted of any crime but was charged by

Jewish leaders with bringing gentiles beyond the Jerusalem Temple barrier to the Jewish area of the Temple complex (Acts 21:33) and for starting riots among Jews based on his preaching (Acts 24:5–8). Roman officials took no action on the case, and eventually Paul appealed to Caesar (Acts 25:11–12) and began a journey to Rome.

For a Roman citizen, to be in chains was utterly shameful and would have caused most people to avoid or reject them. It likely caused some to question whether Paul had God's support as he claimed. With his credibility on the line, Paul explains his calling as God's grace to him, a gift to preach a revealed mystery, namely that gentiles are co-heirs with Jews in Christ. Paul continues with additional details. He is a servant (*diakonos*, from which we get the word *deacon*) of the gospel, which is another way of saying that he received an assignment from God that he has been carrying out. Paul also declares that he is of insignificance, unimportance (3:8), in relation to "the saints" or holy ones (*hagioi*), his typical term for believers (Eph 1:1). Paul speaks in a similar way to the Corinthians, explaining that he is least of the apostles because he persecuted the church (1 Cor 15:9). We should pause to mention that Paul does not talk about struggles with doing the law during his time as Jew, but he does express frustration at the power of sin which prevented him from doing the law, based on his flesh, which was powerless in the end to resist. Romans 7:14–25 describes Paul's life as a Jew under the law, a life that loved the law in his heart but despaired of doing it. Paul describes his Christian experience in Rom 8, a life in Christ, filled with the Holy Spirit.

Ephesians 3:1–7

Paul spends more time talking about his mission given by God. He speaks of the responsibility or administration (*oikonomia*) given him by God as evidence of God's grace (3:2). He says much the same thing a few verses later, when he speaks of the gift of God's grace that Paul received (3:7). It is difficult to determine syntactically whether the emphasis is on Paul's own calling to preach the gospel or on the message preached. But looking at the wider context, Paul probably focuses on both, because his own integrity witnesses to the integrity of the gospel message (see also 1 Cor 11:1).

This gospel message is described as a mystery, by which Paul means something hidden and now revealed (3:3, 4, 8), an idea we also find earlier when Paul describes the mystery of God's will that is now revealed in the plan to bring all things together in Christ (1:9). He speaks of the mystery of the unity of Christ and his body (the church) as represented in the union of husband and wife, one flesh (5:31–32). And he closes his letter with a plea that the Ephesians pray for him, for his bold preaching of the mystery of the gospel (6:19). Mystery has to do with unity, with oneness, with the gospel creating one new humanity. Here in chapter 3, Paul explains that they mystery is that gentiles are co-heirs with Jews who follow Jesus Christ. Gentiles are one body with Jews in Christ, a claim Paul made earlier (2:14–16). This revealed mystery shocks the senses with its multifaceted grace.

Ephesians 3:8–13

In 3:8, Paul comments on God's grace that called him to be an apostle to the gentiles at the time when he was vigorously working to silence the followers of Jesus (Acts 9.1–9; Gal 1:13–17). Paul's comment that he is the least of the followers of Jesus (see also 1 Cor 15:9) is not virtue-signaling humility or a comment in the abstract about human sinfulness; rather, it accurately describes his past persecution of believers (Acts 9:2; Gal 1:13). This grace drew people who were actively disobedient and made them sons and daughters of the most high God. This grace created an inheritance and heirs by adoption. This grace made possible a unity of Jew and gentile followers wherein neither group assimilates the other, but rather all are made new. Paul recognizes that specific group identity markers will remain as characteristic of one's heritage, but he declares that both groups share the promises fulfilled in Christ. His proclamation of unity in the gospel is not a declaration that gentiles must now assimilate to Jewish practices nor that Jews now must throw away their Sabbath rest tradition, for example. It is so easy for the dominant group to insist that their cultural practices are the norm for community life. We face similar challenges today on the mission field, as often the gospel comes pre-packaged in the missionary's own culture.[1]

Paul emphasizes two other important aspects of this grace, its reach to the heavens, and its expression in the church (3:10). First, Paul stresses that this gracious plan of salvation, this mystery now revealed, exemplifies God's wisdom to those rulers and powers that populate the spiritual realm. These forces are likely good and bad and had influence in human

---

1. For an excellent discussion of cross-cultural pitfalls in communicating the gospel, see Richards and O'Brien, *Misreading Scripture with Western Eyes.*

institutions (but should not be conflated with them). God's wisdom can look like weakness, when we think of the cross, for example (1 Cor 1:18, 23–25). But as Paul declares to the Corinthians, God's power is seen in the redemption through Christ, who is our wisdom, our righteousness, and our holiness (1 Cor 1:26–31). The wisdom of God puts human wisdom to shame, with its pursuits of status, ego, and domination. Paul explains that these heavenly rulers get a demonstration of God's wisdom as they see the creation and sustaining of Christ's body, the church.

Second, it is through the church, Christ's body, that God's wisdom shines bright. As Christ's body, the church represents peace and healing and justice to a world under the power of spiritual forces that foment discord and hatred. Paul uses the passive voice of the verb "to make known" to reinforce the point that it is *God's* actions that make known his wisdom. The church is not independently tasked to do so; rather, its very existence testifies to God's wisdom. The church in Paul's day had no triumphal illusions, but over the centuries, when the church has had political power, it has imagined itself to be empowered to make known God's wisdom. To further describe this wisdom, Paul uses an adjective not found elsewhere in the New Testament (*polupoikilos*) and which carries the sense of great variety or diversity (3:10). Through this wisdom, God pursued and accomplished his plan, redemption through Jesus Christ, adoption into God's family.

Wisdom can seem abstract, sterile, heady. God's wisdom is not esoteric, but is relational, it brings relationship through Christ's faithfulness and our faith in Christ Jesus. Paul proclaims that believers have access with complete freedom and acceptance to converse with the God of the universe (3:12; see also 2:18). Paul reinforces God's wisdom in part because God's gift of redemption could seem so unwise based on the standards of the day. Giving such a gift, a grace, to the unimpressive, the broken, the lackluster and average, could seem reckless and foolish. Greco-Roman culture labeled as wise a benefactor or leader who used their resources to benefit productive and promising people. Alternatively, if a gift was given to those seemingly unworthy ones, does that mean the gift is so-so also? Of course not, for this gift allows believers to boldly and with freedom enter God's presence because of Christ. It is this same boldness that he asks for in the Ephesians' prayers for him (6:19).

Paul includes the phrase translated as either "through the faithfulness of Christ" or "through faith in him" (3:12). The question boiling down to whether Paul uses an objective genitive (our faith in Christ) or subjective genitive (Christ's own faithfulness). Those arguing for an objective genitive want to protect the idea that salvation is a free gift of God. On the other side, those promoting a subjective genitive stress Christ's work in establishing redemption. Both ideas are well represented in Paul. The term faith (*pistis*) carried the idea of truth and trustworthiness, loyalty, and a set of beliefs. A person could be trustworthy and could believe something was true. Believers express faith by their loyalty to Christ and his work, which likewise demonstrated loyalty to the redemption plan established within the Trinity before the foundation of the world (1:4).

Paul concludes this section with "therefore" (3:13) and follows with the enigmatic statement that his sufferings in chains are "for them" and are "your glory." He indicated in 3:1 that his chains are "for them," and he uses the same clause here, that his afflictions are "for them." What the world calls shameful, Paul declares glorious, for the chains are a direct result of his faithful testimony about the work of God for salvation. The chains become honorable because they witness to the power of God to bring salvation to gentiles. The Ephesians share this glory as members of God's family (2:19), as part of God's temple (2:22), and as those seated with Christ in the heavenly places (2:6). Rome seeks to project its power with chains, to squelch dissent with its domination. Those in power use custody to maintain the status quo, and to enhance their own control. Paul's letters and Acts make clear that God's gospel word is unchained, unrestricted, unhindered in its effectiveness, and Roman power, or any earthly power, is unable to restrain it.

Ephesians 3:1–13: Reflections for Preaching and Teaching

When bad things happen to trustworthy authorities, people can question the rightness of their message. Think of Job's friends, who were certain that Job had some unconfessed sin that was the root cause of his sufferings. Two big, overlapping ideas emerge from this passage, one theological, one practical. First the practical: pastors and teachers who face suffering and setbacks might be viewed with suspicion by others. Paul sets the example here. On the one hand, leaders can assure their community that the difficult situation is the result of faithfully following God's call and walking through the spiritual resistance that such faithfulness creates. On the other hand, the congregation can learn from Paul's challenge to the Ephesians that struggles and obstacles are part of the Christian walk and do not necessarily indicate God's displeasure.

Second, the theological: obey faithfully in whatever capacity God has called you, for God equips and supports each believer. The immense riches of Christ, the bold freedom to approach God, and the knowledge that a believer's fidelity demonstrates God's gracious wisdom to the spiritual powers, these truths reframe the trials and struggles as part of God's larger mission.

There is a third idea that implicitly emerges from this passage, namely the challenge to those who have the power or resources to alleviate suffering or correct injustice. Paul does not expect his tiny congregation to advocate to a Roman judge on his behalf; the power differential is too great.[2] However, the peace and unity that comes with being in Christ mandates that those with influence use it for the good of the whole and for the sake of the vulnerable. First-century believers had no political muscle, no social capital, no grassroots cultural movement to help address the abuse of power that Rome exercised, including beatings and imprisonments. But the church today in many places does have opportunities and resources to address injustices, including the prison systems, a relevant example for this passage.

The United States has one of the highest incarceration rates in the world, with 2.2 million men and women behind bars.[3] There are about 4,500 prison facilities across the U.S., an uptick of 400 percent capacity since 1980. Moreover, the racial disparities revealed in the numbers indicates a systemic racism underpinning the penal system. African Americans are seven times as likely as whites to be imprisoned, and Hispanics are three times as likely to be imprisoned as whites.[4] What are some tools from Scripture that we can use to think about our own part in this reality?

How do we do justice better? First, we can examine our own situatedness and biases. This provides a baseline for reflecting, and by getting our assumptions out on the table, we can allow God's word to challenge them. Paul stresses to the Ephesians the trinitarian love that enacts a redemptive plan that redeems from sins and creates a new community in Christ, with

---

2. There were very few buildings in the ancient world set aside to hold prisoners. Paul relied on others to care for him, for officials were not required to care for prisoners' basic needs. Jesus and the apostles encouraged believers to care for those in custody, for they are dependent on the mercy of others (Matt 25:31–46; Heb 13:1–3; 34; and the Philippian church's gift to Paul, Phil 2:25).

3. Skinner, "Remember My Chains," 279.

4. Campbell, "Mass Incarceration," 283.

believers as God's beloved children. Each believer is being transformed daily, putting on the new self (4:20–24).

Second, when we think of prison, we think of punishment, as in, paying for one's crimes. This leads naturally to questions about how much and what sort of punishment fits the crime, or might deter the crime, and who gets to determine punishment and to enforce these decisions?[5] A problem this big has no easy fixes, but we can be sure that a solution will require changes in attitudes and advantages of those for whom the system seems to work just fine. It requires a rethinking of our tendency to consider the guilty as deserving their shame, for this reasoning tricks believers into imagining that they need not follow Jesus's call to show compassion to those in custody.

Third, no one is beyond the reach of redemption, so how do we instantiate that conviction into real policies and practices? Community and national groups exist to help those currently in prison and those re-entering their communities. Christians can get involved with policy making at the local, state, and national level. Perhaps most importantly, believers can visit prisons. They will find other believers there already, other Christian communities, and indeed, they will see that God is already working in prisons, as he is everywhere and in all communities. Amy-Jill Levine writes of her years teaching at the Riverbend Maximum Security Institute, a prison located near Vanderbilt, where she taught her "insider students" for many years. She declares that these students, whom she calls her friends, "have taught me, repeatedly, that they are individual, with families and friends, with stories of how they came to be sentenced to prison, with guilt and remorse. As one remarked, . . . We are human beings, just like you, in the image and likeness of God."[6] Levine invites readers to ponder the reality of the two men crucified on either side of Jesus, as their stories are ones "with which we should wrestle, stories of crime and punishment, of anguish and hope, of blasphemy and salvation."[7]

---

5. Gilliard, *Rethinking Incarceration*, 22, recounts one example of the "three strikes and you're out" law, which disproportionately affects men and women of color, wherein a woman was sentenced to over ten years for writing five bad checks, none of which exceeded $150.00. Three that bounced were to Toys 'R' Us for Christmas gifts for her children.

6. Levine, *Witness at the Cross*, 28.

7. Levine, *Witness at the Cross*, 35.

Ephesians 3:14–21:
Paul's Prayer to Know Christ's Love Deeply

Paul encourages believers to approach God in prayer with boldness and confidence (3:12). He then models that assurance in our passage wherein he writes an audacious prayer that ends with the request that believers be filled with God's fullness. Having made clear in the first part of the chapter the mystery now revealed (namely, that gentiles are partakers of the promises in Christ), Paul now prays that this reality—which shakes the heavenly realm with its wisdom—will likewise completely infuse their whole person. Earlier in the epistle, Paul prayed that the Ephesians would understand their inheritance in Christ, secured by God's resurrection power (1:17–19).

Paul invites us to imagine him kneeling as he brings his request to the Father. Paul opened this letter with praise to the Father of the Lord Jesus Christ and further described God as the Father of glory (1:3, 17). Paul uses "Abba, Father" to address God (Rom 8:15; Gal 4:6), and I should note that the Aramaic "abba" does not mean "daddy" in the child-like way a toddler calls to her dad. Nevertheless, it is a term of relationship, as Jesus addresses his Father in his great moment of need in the Garden of Gethsemane (Mark 14:36). Here in 3:14, Paul stresses the Father's family, which offers alliteration in Greek: Father is *pater*, and family is *patria*. Paul emphasizes that God's fatherhood covers all people, all languages, all cultures, all locations, through all time. James too speaks of the Father in this way, when he describes God the Father as the one who gives good gifts, who is unchanging, and who created all things (1:16–18).

The cosmic reach of God's fatherhood embraces the new gentile believers, who are encouraged to bring their prayers to him. What a contrast from these gentiles' earlier experiences in prayer to their deities. Pagan prayers venerated the deity, included votive offerings, and meticulously followed rules for gestures and actions during prayers, such as touching the ground or altar, lifting an arm to heaven, washing hands, or covering the head (Roman men covered their heads during prayer). Their prayers were not done with confidence or boldness, for the deities did not disclose what pleased them. Nor did the prayers seek to create a caring, loving relationship between the devotee and deity. Paul's prayers, by contrast, highlight God's immeasurable love for his creation, including humanity. The redemption through Christ brings forgiveness of sins and the adoption into God's family as a co-heir with Christ. The relationship established with God by those who are in Christ can be nurtured only through divine power, the Father, Son, and Holy Spirit abiding in ever deepening, thickening ways.

As we reflect on the content of Paul's prayers for the Ephesians, it is interesting to look at Paul's time in Ephesus as described in Acts 19:1–40 as possible background for his prayers. First, we find much evidence of the activity of the Holy Spirit in Ephesus. For example, Paul baptizes certain disciples in Jesus's name and places his hands on them to receive the Holy Spirit (19:6). These believers spoke in tongues and prophesied, demonstrating the presence of the Spirit in them.

Second, God's great power that raised Jesus from the dead was evident in numerous healings and exorcisms (Acts 19:11; Eph 1:19–20). This power was associated with the name of Jesus, a name that Paul tells us in Ephesians is above every name that has been named (1:21). In Jesus's name, Paul drove out demons as part of his apostolic ministry. When others sought to mimic Paul's deeds by using Jesus's name in an exorcism, they were overcome by demonic forces themselves (19:16). This event made such an impression on the inhabitants of Ephesus that those who heard of it held Jesus's name in high honor. Even more, some took the giant step to confess Jesus as Lord. As evidence of their conversion, they burn their magic scrolls. Not only was this act a financially ruinous one, it was a religiously subversive one too. Artemis of the Ephesians seems to have been linked to magical incantations, the *Ephesia grammata*, with an incantation engraved at the base of her statue offering protection to her devotees (Pausanias, in Eustathius, *Comm ad Hom* 19.247).

Ironically, Demetrius saw the danger of Paul's message more clearly than did the town clerk. Why buy images of the goddess for protection when you are sealed with the Holy Spirit? Why honor Artemis when Christ Jesus promises life eternal, having conquered even death? The gospel message upended the Roman pagan social and religious world. The gospel promised inheritances for slaves, wisdom for the poor, love of God to those the city had concluded were unlovable. Paul's prayers emphasize the importance of knowing who God is and who you are in Christ. The opposition against such a loving God who cares for all was strong then, as Acts 19 indicates. And it remains strong as Paul tells us throughout Ephesians, the spiritual forces of darkness are ever present, ever eager to sidetrack and derail believers from their calling. Persevere in prayer, that is Paul's answer.

Ephesians 3:14–19

The content of Paul's request is clear, even if the syntax of this eighty-six-word sentence is not always so apparent (3:14–19). Paul asks the Father to give out of his abundant riches, so there is no question that God has the resources to meet Paul's requests (3:16). The prayer has three main sections, each beginning with "that" (*hina*, 3:16, 18, 19). The three sections are related in one of two ways, either the first clause states the prayer (3:16–17), with the other two clauses providing the desired results, namely that believers have power to grasp the magnitude of the love with surpasses knowledge, and that believers may be filled with God's fullness. Or it is possible each of the clauses contains a specific request. In the end, the grammar evidence is inconclusive on the nature of the three clauses' relationship, but regarding the content and effect of the prayer, we are on much surer footing.

Looking closely at 3:16, Paul asks God to grant strength to believers. This strength comes from God's riches, and the strength manifests as power in one's core being or self, flowing through the Holy Spirit. The power is that which raised Jesus from the dead (1:19–20) and which convinces of Christ's infinite love towards his body, and the world. This is Holy Spirit power, given to renew the mindset of believers. The inner self or inner being is a phrase Paul uses to describe that part of him that delights in God's law (Rom 7:22–23), over against the part of him that resists God's will and succumbs to fleshly desires. He recounts to the Corinthians that his "inner man" is being renewed, even as his outer man is wasting away as one might look who is starving (2 Cor 4:16; see also Col 3:10). This dichotomy within the self represents the reality that believers live *both* in the present, temporary, evil age (Gal 1:4) *and* with Christ in the heavenlies, raised and seated with him (Eph 2:6).

The strengthening of the inner self through the Holy Spirit is to allow for the indwelling of Christ in an ever-deepening way (3:17; see also Col 1:27). The verb "to dwell" carries the sense of settling down, inhabiting a space. Paul uses the related noun in 2:22 describing the dwelling place made up of believers in which God lives. The reference to "hearts" likely parallels the inner self noted in the previous verse. Likewise, the phrases "through the Spirit" and "through faith." The heart is the seat of physical, intellectual, and spiritual life, not only the place of emotions as we think of it today. Paul continues describing Christ's dwelling with an additional phrase that believers would cultivate the reality that they are rooted and grounded in God's love. Paul uses perfect passive participles, which convey the sense that something happened in the past that continues in the present. There is both a positional and an experiential point being made. Believers have been established in Christ, adopted into God's family, redeemed from sin, sealed with the Holy Spirit, as we saw in chapter 1. Paul now emphasizes the experiential aspect of the redemption plan, namely, that believers embrace Christ's indwelling in their hearts through continuingly exercising their faith in him and his love.

Christ's love is cemented securely in a believer's heart; the foundation is unassailable. But while that is true, it might not always *feel* true, and so Paul's prayer continues as he focuses on broadening the imagination of believers as to the expansive magnificence of God's love. Paul asks that believers receive God's power to understand with their whole self the extent of Christ's love. And this is not a data dump, nor can it be captured in a proposition, or a single event. It is a lifelong and daily openness to experience the radical complexity of Christ's love for us. Christ is *for* us, each one of us.

In 3:18, we have the second of three sections, as Paul declares that the believers might have the ability or power to understand what by all accounts is incomprehensible, at least to the unaided human mind. The love described is essentially indescribable, but its perception is not limited to elite intellectuals or mystics or special revelation. Such incomprehensible comprehension is available to all believers, and it consists of one thing: love. This love has no boundaries, extending beyond the limits of the cosmos. We are encouraged to know a love that is beyond knowledge—a seeming contradiction that is resolved when we recall that we as creatures are finite, but God is infinite. This love can take up space, if you will, in that it can fill us with God's fullness (3:19). In the final section of the prayer, Paul asks that believers be filled fully with God's fullness. Paul indicated in 1:23 that the church, Christ's body, is the fullness, likely of Christ. He says that Christ fills all things, including his body. And now in chapter 3, Paul prays that what is true will affect their daily experiences, that Christ's love is all sufficient; it never ends, it never fails (1 Cor 13:8). I think Paul really believed this; do we?

Ephesians 3:20–21

Paul ends his prayer with a doxology that praises the God the Father and honors Christ and his body, the church. Here, as throughout the prayer, Paul focuses on God's power as able to accomplish his purposes (see also

Rom 16:25). Paul contrasts God's immeasurable power with believers' limited capacity to understand their situation and even imagine all that they have in Christ. This truth is comforting, for it releases believers from having to know what to ask God, for God has in mind greater things than we can envision. Paul continues that this power works in us. Most likely Paul alludes to the Holy Spirit that upholds and supports believers as they pray and meditate on God's amazing love in Christ.

Ephesians 3:14–21: Reflections for Preaching and Teaching

Who is God in this passage? Who am I, based on this passage? These are always excellent questions to ask but are vital in this case. Paul captures in a single paragraph the essentials of our trinitarian God and how that God interacts with humanity. God is Father, which means humanity is his family. God is Spirit, which allows for each person to be strengthened at their very core. God is Christ, who dwells in believers, confirming the unfathomable, immeasurable love that fills them to overflowing. The result of answering these two questions is the celebration of God's glory and power.

It should not be forgotten that Paul pens these words while in chains. If ever there was a time to urge God to use his power to free his servant, this would seem like such a time. We have no evidence that Paul did this. However, he does share a request that God answered in an unexpected way. In 2 Corinthians, Paul recounts a powerful vision he had of things inexpressible (12:1–10). This great revelation was followed by a "messenger from Satan," an enigmatic phrase that has puzzled readers ever since. Whatever the problem, Paul pleaded with God to have it go away, and God did not respond with a "yes." Instead, God showed his power by allowing Paul to rely on his grace and not on his own sense of self-worth. Paul later realized that his prayer would quite probably have led to arrogance, and so he embraced the weakness that came from the messenger from Satan. Paul rejoiced in his own weakness, for God's strength in him is strong. What good news that God will do more than we ask, for we do not always ask well. What joy that God's power works in his church, empowering the good works he prepared in advance (2:10). What amazing love that believers celebrate in Jesus Christ.

Paul's Prayers in Ephesians chapters 1, 3, and 6

Paul's prayers in chapters 1, 3, and 6, provide a window into God's redemption plan as Paul applies his theology in prayer over the Ephesian believers. His prayers might surprise us today in their lack of specificity about circumstances and their lofty language. A temptation for believers is to skip lightly over the praise part of prayer and spend time in a long list of needs and wants. Paul teaches us to ground our prayers in trinitarian reality, in salvation truth, and in new life in Christ. As we move through the prayers, we will focus on Paul's description of God the Father, Son, and Holy Spirit. We will attend to God's actions and character, which leads to a reflection on believers' redemption. Paul's prayers focus on *who* believers are in Christ. Elsewhere in this letter, Paul develops *what* believers should do based on their redeemed status in Christ, which connects back to the language of his prayers. He makes this clear in his personal prayer request at the end of the letter. There we find his theologically grounded prayer applied to his own faithfulness to God's calling.

The letter to the Ephesians contains exalted, trinitarian language about God that, not surprisingly, is on full display in the prayers. Paul addresses his prayers to God the Father of glory, also translated as "glorious Father." Paul speaks of God the Father of the Lord Jesus Christ in his opening lines to the Ephesians (1:3), and perhaps Paul draws on this truth to stress that God is Father of the One (Jesus Christ) who brings glory to his Father (see 1 Cor 2:8). More likely, however, Paul stresses the characteristic "glory" that belongs to God. Earlier in chapter 1, Paul offers the phrase "to the praise of his glory" three times, and he will repeat the term "glory" twice in his prayer in chapter 3. Why an emphasis on God's glory? With this term, Paul captures the all-surpassing greatness and love of God, the sort that only the Creator has and that creatures should happily celebrate. Such glory contains great power, and Paul emphasizes that God exercises such power on our behalf. Additionally, God's glory displays beauty and majesty, from awe-inspiring sunsets to the exquisiteness of a newborn baby. This Father, Paul adds in chapter 3, is the Father of every family, that is, all humanity past, present, and future. The connection is reinforced in the Greek, with father—*pater*—and family—*patria*—making a verbal link in the listeners' ears. Here in chapter 3, Paul picks up his recent insistence that his imprisonment is for the sake of gentile believers' glory. Implied by Paul is the truth that God is not only the God of the Jews; rather, he is the Creator God, the one true God for *all* peoples, for all time.

From his position as Father of all, God the Father has glorious riches that he chooses to give. No more precious gift can be given than that of our salvation in Christ. In chapter 1, Paul identifies the Lord Jesus Christ's Father as the one to whom he prays. This is the Lord Jesus in whom the believers have placed their faith (1:15). This same Jesus was raised from the dead and now is seated in the place of greatest honor, at the right hand of his Father (1:20). Paul slides from his specific prayer seamlessly into a further description of Christ as the one who has all things under his feet and is head over all things. This all for the sake of the church, his body.

Paul's prayer in chapter 3 individualizes this truth by attending to each believer's inner self in Christ. Paul explains that Christ dwells by faith in each believer's heart and then focuses on how such love can be anchored in this in-dwelling love. The believer's heart is the seat not only of emotions, but of will and rational thought; it is the center of the person. Paul indicates that Christ's love is beyond human comprehension (3:19), as the Creator's thoughts are beyond the creatures' understanding. Paul includes a string of four nouns representing dimensions of space—wide, long, high, deep, which likely refer to the immeasurable capacity of Christ's love. It is also possible that Paul implies the work of Christ's cross (Augustine, Jerome) or points the spotlight on God the Father's love (Chrysostom). And perhaps Paul is deliberately vague, wanting readers to imagine the entire salvation plan, established before time and encompassing the entire cosmos.

The Holy Spirit plays a central role in both prayers. Paul asks that the Ephesians receive the Spirit of wisdom and revelation (1:17), which will lead to knowing God more deeply. A few qualifications should be noted. First, believers already enjoy the Holy Spirit's indwelling, and they are sealed by the Spirit (1:13–14). Paul asks here that the Spirit would be actively building strong relational ties between the believer and his or her God. Pause for a moment here, the focus is on *relationship*, not what you can or must do for God or what God can or should do for you. This is not about transactions, but relationships, facilitated by the Spirit through whom flows God's power into believers' hearts. The Holy Spirit remains on believers as a seal, assuring them of their inheritance in Christ (1:14).

The mention of inheritance leads us to the second topic of focus, namely, what does Paul ask of the Father? In chapter 1, Paul requests three things related to believers' lives: their hope, their inheritance, and God's power at work for them. First, Paul asks that believers might know "the hope of their calling." Paul emphasizes both "hope" and "calling" in chapter

4 (4:1, 4); here, Paul introduces the subjects. Hope in Paul does not reflect uncertainty, but rather that salvation has not been fully realized, for Christ's second coming and the drawing together of all things in Christ (1:10) have not yet happened. Paul asks God that the community better understand their "calling," which has been established by God before the world was created (1:4), that they would be adopted as God's children through Christ's work of redemption. Paul makes a similar claim to the Romans, as he explains that those whom God predestined, he also called and justified and glorified (Rom 8:30). In both cases, Paul does not take up the philosophical questions around human free will, which were active among Jews and gentile thinkers of his day. Instead, Paul emphasizes the sure promise of God's redemption, the hope of their calling in Christ.

Second, Paul asks that believers know the full extent of their inheritance as God's people. Paul understands salvation to be more than forgiveness of sins, as it includes being part of God's family. Paul earlier stressed that believers are adopted through Christ Jesus (1:5), and as a family member, one receives an inheritance. I will say more about this in chapter 6, but it bears mentioning here that for most of the Ephesians, there was little to inherit from a human standpoint. If we assume that 20 percent were slaves, then they were sure to get nothing unless their owners willed it to them at their death.[8] And most believers would be poor, shopkeepers or artisans, workers at the docks or in bakeries. They had few resources saved, maybe a week's wages. They might pass down their shop or skill to their son or daughter, but the children would not inherit lands or wealth. Paul repeatedly speaks of salvation as adoption into God's family, which carries riches and honor beyond any human imagination, to say nothing of the joyful delight of being part of the family of saints in Christ.

Third, Paul speaks of an aspect of God's power, namely its immeasurable greatness. Paul further explains this greatness as God's power raising Jesus from the dead. The power is used to bring life, to defeat death. It would be no surprise to the Ephesians that God is powerful. They were

---

8. Mouritsen writes, "manumission was both very common and very selective." Mouritsen, *Freedman in the Roman World*, 140. He suggests that "between a quarter and a third of the households may have been freed at any time." Mouritsen, *Freedman in the Roman World*, 139. Perry concludes, "By prioritizing marriage and reproduction as grounds for manumission and citizenship, historians and lawmakers in the early Principate not only rewarded the female slaves fulling these roles, but also asserted that these activities had value and were citizenlike." Perry, *Gender, Manumission, and the Roman Freedwoman*, 66.

raised in an environment that celebrated Artemis of the Ephesians, who lived in a temple that was four times the size of the Parthenon in Athens. She defended the city and protected women in childbirth; one could say that she was celebrated for bringing safety and life. But God in Christ does more—death is defeated, and eternal life is gained through Christ.

The subjects of power and strength are picked up again at the beginning of Paul's prayer in chapter 3. Here Paul asks that God might give believers strength with power, with the ability to fully express the inner self and fully welcome Christ's indwelling in their hearts. This inner person is a new creation in Christ (2 Cor 5:17; Gal 2:20); he or she is a member of Christ's body, a piece of God's temple now being built, a sibling to all other believers in Christ. God's power feels like a loving embrace, as the strength given through his glorious riches empowers worship. The power sows love, grows love, confirms love. The power invites reflection on the magnitude of God's love and encourages experiencing such love and relying daily on such love. The result is that God's fullness would fill believers (3:19), even as Christ fills the church (1:22–23).

Paul continues that such power is working in believers, such that God provides beyond what we could even think to ask (3:20). This does not mean that God gives people what they want or desire; Paul does not advocate a "health and wealth" message, or prosperity gospel. Paul sees God's work in believers' lives promoting holiness, blamelessness (1:4), furthering a lifestyle that reflects God's kingdom values (5:3–6). Lest any believer be in despair that they could not "measure up" to God's ideal, Paul reassures all of us that his power—the same that raised Jesus from the dead and encompasses all love—that power promises to make us mature in Christ (4:15).

Paul makes a prayer request at the end of the letter, right after encouraging the Ephesians to pray often for each other and other needs. Paul modeled this posture of prayer for others in his earlier prayers. His charge to pray is grammatically linked to his discussion of the armor of God, but it is probably not part of the armor itself. Instead, Paul reflects the battle environment in which the believer puts on the armor of God, which requires active communication with the Holy Spirit. Four times in 4:18, Paul repeats "all" as he insists that they make "all kinds" of prayers at "all times" with "all" perseverance for "all" believers.

Paul asks for their prayers, that he would be faithful to the mission God gave him. He asks for prayer that he would be bold, fearless, in his proclamation. Along with boldness, he asks that his testimony would be clear and compelling, that those listening would understand the mystery. This mystery has been explained earlier in the epistle as the gospel message that gentiles are co-heirs with Jews in Christ (3:6) and are in God's family created through Christ (2:19). This mystery includes the union of Christ and his church (5:32).

EPHESIANS 4

Ephesians 4:1–16: Walk Worthy of Your Calling

PAUL BEGAN THIS LETTER with the declaration of praise that God chose to adopt believers in Christ to be holy and blameless. Here in chapter 4, Paul begins to get specific on what holiness and blamelessness looks like and how believers can live into this calling. In both 4:1 and 4:17, Paul asks that believers walk (or live) in worthiness before God. This worthiness is not based on one's own capacity for success, or one's natural talents, or even on the evaluation of society or family. Living worthy of the gospel is living by faith, being obedient, stepping out to do those good works that are waiting to be done, because God prepared them for you to do (2:10). Believers need to know how to act in their new family, what the expectations are, and what pleases the Father.

Paul reminds readers of the unity that Christ made, as through the cross he created one new humanity by destroying the enmity between Jew and gentile, bringing peace. This unity, however, does not mean sameness. As a body has different organs and limbs, so too the church requires differentiation to be healthy. The point is that in unity, no one is more valuable than another (see also 1 Cor 12:12–26). This new humanity, his body, is to grow and mature, equipped by Christ and speaking truth in love. With confessional conciseness and poetic phrases, Paul summarizes the life available to the believer.

Ephesians 4:1–6

The first six verses of this chapter make up a single sentence in Greek and stress the unity or oneness of the gospel message. Paul puts in front of them his chains again (see also 3:1), probably to reinforce his own example of living out his calling. Christ Jesus called Paul to be an apostle to the gentiles (Acts 9:1–9; see also Gal 1:15); living out that call meant hardships and imprisonments. Paul is not asking the Ephesians to do anything he is unwilling to do himself.

Twice in the first verse, Paul mentions "call," as a noun and as a verb: the calling to which you have been called. The call comes from God and is sustained by God's power (see also Rom 8:30). Nevertheless, believers must step into the calling. Paul uses the verb "to walk" which is often translated as "to live"; the translation clearly represents the verb's meaning, but it might lack the force and visual image of a believer moving through the day, making decisions that reflect God's values. Previously, the gentile believers had walked under the influence of the ruler of this world, now they are to walk on a new path. Paul repeats this call to walk in 4:17. We see the use of "walk" as "living faithfully" in the well-known verse of Ps 23, that as David walks through the valley of the shadow of death, he does not fear, for God is with him.[1]

We might brush past 4:2, for we are used to hearing about humility and patience as Christian virtues. But the earliest listeners would have paused, for these virtues could threaten their social status. The first listed, "humility," would be better translated as humiliation, for no free man at this time would express humility—that trait was expected of those who were below him. And the same could be said as well of female slave owners towards their male slaves. Paul follows here the Old Testament teaching that God exalts the humble (Isa 11:4; 49:13; 66:2; Prov 3:34; see also 1 Pet 5:5; Jas 1:9–10). In first-century Ephesus, however, asking each believer to treat others with humbleness was a radical social move, countercultural. Nevertheless, it was also what Jesus modeled so often, including the washing of his disciples' feet (John 13). Even as Peter was horrified at the thought of Jesus washing his feet, so too I imagine some Ephesian believers questioned in their hearts whether they could manage this.

Jesus demonstrates these qualities and assures his followers that he is gentle and humble (Matt 11:29–30). With Jesus as our role model and with his love residing deep in our hearts, believers have the God-given power to behave in a worthy manner before their Father and their siblings in Christ. Patience and gentleness require self-control and an outward focus. Demonstrating these virtues requires others both to give patience and humble service and to receive it. These virtues support and sustain unity of the group.

1. Green, *Conversion in Luke–Acts*, 65.

To be clear, this unity is not created by the church; it is God's creation through Christ's work on the cross. Paul declared earlier that Christ is our peace, and here he speaks of the bonds of peace which hold the community together. The term "bonds" is related to the term for "chains" that hold Paul. In both cases, these bonds are not evidence of restrictions or punishment, but of joyful peace in participating in Christ's life.

Directly after stating the term "peace," Paul speaks of one body and one spirit. Juxtaposing these terms reinforces his earlier claims that Christ is our peace and has created one new humanity in himself (2:14–15). The church is his body (1:22–23) and is enlivened and sustained by the Holy Spirit (2:22). Paul continues in 4:4 to stress their identity as people called by God in Christ by stating both the noun "call" and the verb "to call," repeating the emphasis from 4:1. Paul does not typically use this noun and verb together, but its repetition here fits the letter's rhetorical flourish evident throughout its six chapters. Here, Paul connects calling and hope as he had earlier done in his prayer that the Ephesians appreciate this gift of redemption and new creation that is theirs in Christ (1:18). Elsewhere, Paul encourages the Romans that the gifts and calling of God are irrevocable (Rom 11:29), a sure hope because God has established it.

Paul continues with three nouns, each preceded by the word "one." One Lord, *kyrios*, referring to the Lord Jesus Christ. The OT uses this term to refer to God, and Paul uses it extensively to identify Jesus the Son (4:13), the one who is fully God with the Father and the Holy Spirit. Paul speaks of Jesus as Lord in a confessional sense (Rom 10:9; 14:8–9; 1 Cor 8:6: Phil 2:9–11). The Greek term can also refer to a slave owner, and Paul uses it that way in 6:5–9. Not only one Lord, there is also one faith. Paul refers here to what the church later refers to as the rule of faith, the beliefs that the church confesses. Paul speaks of the "word of truth" and the "gospel of salvation" (1:13), which convey the meaning of "one faith." With one Lord and one faith, there is one baptism (see also 1 Cor 12:13). Paul likely has in mind here the liturgical act of using water to baptize a follower. It can also carry a metaphorical sense of participating in Christ's death (Rom 6:4; Col 2:12), and Paul might want both to be operating here.

Paul closes this poetic confessional by celebrating the one God and Father. Paul stresses God's oneness rather infrequently, which might indicate it was taken for granted by both Jew and gentile, the latter familiar with the Jewish claims about their God. When Paul speaks of God's oneness, typically he also mentions the Holy Spirit and Jesus Christ, as he does here.

Paul does not use the term "Trinity," but his descriptions of the Godhead are trinitarian. God is identified as Father of all. Earlier, God was identified as the Father of the Lord Jesus Christ and as father of all people, and now as father of all. Paul likely points to the Father's care of his entire world and of all humans and certainly his special care of believers in Christ. The all-encompassing care of God the Father over the entire cosmos makes the hope to which believers are called absolutely secure.

Ephesians 4:7–16

Having made the importance of unity and oneness crystal clear, Paul turns to explaining how Christ accomplishes this oneness in his church. Paul expands the metaphor of the church as body, growing to maturity. The Lord Jesus with the Father gives a gift to his church, a tool set that delivers the means to build acts of service that bless both the church and the wider world. The tools include teaching and evangelizing resources that strengthen believers. Interestingly, Paul does not mention the Holy Spirit here nor does he speak about spiritual gifts, but a single gift from Christ to his church. In Romans and 1 Corinthians, Paul speaks about gifts (*charismata*), with the emphasis on individual believers' special gifting by the Holy Spirit (Rom 12:3–8; 1 Cor 12:4–11).

Ephesians 4:11–16 are a single sentence in Greek. Paul stresses unity based on Christ's gift of empowering his church through resources of teaching and evangelizing, to do those good works created by God for the church to do (Eph 2:10). This gift is given for the benefit of all believers; it is not describing gifts of leadership given to certain members of the body nor is Paul establishing a specific church structure. Those who read this passage as focused on individual leaders insert the verb "to be" before each noun. However, the emphasis is on the duties themselves (evangelizing, teaching, etc.), not on the people exercising the gift. Paul includes as part of the gift to the church, apostles, prophets, evangelists, pastors (shepherds), and teachers. In much the same way, Paul explains his apostleship to the Corinthians as being their servant, with God giving the growth (1 Cor 3:6–9). In all five cases, the primary function is the accurate telling of the gospel message, explaining the will of God to the people of God and to society. We have examples of women apostles (Rom 16:7), prophets (Acts 21:9), and teachers (Acts 18:26), and Priscilla and Aquila led the Ephesian church.

Paul cites Ps 68:18 to highlight Christ's finished work in establishing God's victory, a future hope to which the psalmist pointed. The psalm speaks of God *receiving* gifts from people, while Ephesians writes that he (Christ) *gave* gifts to people. Later rabbinic tradition cites the psalm as referring to Moses who learned Torah and then gave it as a gift to people. This evidence is much later than Paul, who moreover does not speak about Moses in this passage. More likely, Paul saw this psalm fulfilled in Christ's work of victory over his enemies, including death.

The psalm celebrates God establishing himself and his temple in Jerusalem on Mt. Zion. God is the divine warrior, the one who establishes justice and receives gifts, likely from Israel to build the temple. The psalmist rejoices in God's victory over rulers, a theme that Paul emphasizes with Christ's work (1:20–21; 3:10; 6:12, 16). Finally, this specific quotation from Ps 68 stresses the ascension, a point that Paul underlines. Christ is seated at God the Father's right hand, and believers are seated with Christ in the heavens (1:20; 2:6; see also Acts 2:32–35). Christ reigns victorious over his enemies, over all powers of evil, by taking them captive. Paul speaks of believers attaining to the fullness of Christ (2:13), which reinforces the image of the church as a temple filled with God's presence (2 Chr 5:13–14; 7:1–3; Ezek 43:1–5).

Not only does Christ ascend, but Paul stresses that he descended to the lower regions. Most likely he refers to the earth here, lower in relation to the heavens. He points to the incarnation of Christ Jesus (see also Phil 2:6–11). Had Paul wanted to refer to hell, he could have used terms such as Hades or "the abyss" (Rom 10:7). Moreover, Paul is not speaking here of the descent of the Holy Spirit at Pentecost.

The goal for the body of Christ is to speak the truth in love (4:15), to speak accurately about the gospel, and to live in line with that gospel message. Paul's discussions about speaking truth in love in his other letters are quite instructive. Paul separates the pure gospel message from any personal attacks against his situation. He indicates to the Philippians that some preach out of envy and rivalry, as he is in chains, but he does not care so long as Christ is preached (Phil 1). Yet to the Corinthians, he is adamant that the personal attacks against him should not be dismissed. The reason for this seeming contradiction is that those personal attacks are rooted in a false picture of the gospel. Paul declares that he cannot speak the gospel with worldly rhetoric or human wisdom, for to do so would empty the cross of its power—an amazing statement! Paul insists that Christ's work makes a single body of fellowship that does not privilege Jew over gentile, or gentile over Jew. When a decision does impact unity, as Peter's did in Antioch, then Paul declares such a decision to be wrong (Gal 2:11–22).

Second, speaking the truth in love requires that believers love, even as they uphold the truth. Nowhere is this stated more soberly than in Revelation when the angel of the church of Ephesus remonstrates the believers. The angel praises believers for their hard work and perseverance, their testing of teachings to know what is true. Then the hammer falls, and the angel declares that they have lost or abandoned (*aphiēmi*) their first love. As such, they are in danger of losing their lampstand, which is their identity as Christ's church, if they do not repent. Knowing truth is not enough, the church must walk in love as Christ loves. How might we believers avoid the dangers of abandoning our first love? I suggest that to retain this love, believers must focus on the church as Christ's body. We saw above in 4:1–6 the call to live into our oneness in Christ as his body: one Lord, one faith, one baptism. As a member of Christ's body, we are being built up, and this finds expression in acts of service (4:12). Paul likely has in mind both works that help fellow believers, but also works that bless their pagan neighbors, hopefully so that they become followers of Jesus.

Ephesians 4:1–16: Reflections for Preaching and Teaching

Paul's defining message in this passage can be summarized in one word: *one*. The central redemptive claims are one Lord, one faith, one baptism. The main visual image is of the universal church as one human body, with Christ as head. The one goal of each believer is emulating Christ. The key marker that demonstrates worthy living is the oneness of the body, a unity in the faith. Today, we hear "one" and think "individual," but oneness for Paul's first-century listeners included community. The mature believer is the one who expresses humility, patience, service, and truth-telling in love, all of which require other people as recipients of these attitudes and behaviors.

There are at least three ways we can live into the one-body reality reflected in acts of service. First, by reframing social codes to align with the gospel. Second, by reckoning our shared humanity, and not only with other believers but with unbelievers too. Third, by living into our head, Christ, and his self-sacrificial love (5:2).

It might seem odd at first glance to focus on social mores when discussing transcendent values such as truth and love. Nevertheless, it is precisely in our daily lives that these ultimate values are put into practice. In Paul's life, the emphasis on truth in love played out in Ephesus, in the story of the near riot instigated by Demetrius the silversmith (Acts 19:23–41). Recall that Demetrius took offense at Paul's message, worried that his own trade in Artemis idols would be diminished. He was afraid of income loss, the decreased status of his business, and the reduced reputation of the goddess. That day in Ephesus, he led the unrest, as townspeople shouted, "Great is Artemis of the Ephesians!" (Acts 19:34). The small band of believers faced a great challenge, namely, how they could both deal with the wrath of the multitude and speak the truth in love.

The gospel came with great power, evidenced by healings and other miracles. Both Jews and gentiles in Ephesus were in fear and awe, and many sought the Lord, repenting of their sins. They burned books of magical spells; these actions are a clear testimony to the belief in the power of Christ over any other spiritual force.

However, this power also threatens the pagan community. Fear of a different sort rears its head. Those whose livelihood relies directly on the cult of Artemis raise the alarm. They defend their own way of life, the honoring of Artemis and Rome, and all the entailments that go along with this. One entailment is the imperial propaganda that stressed the *pax Romana*, the peace of Rome. This faux peace was achieved through a highly stratified society and tightly held social ranking that apportioned out varying amounts of social worth to individuals depending on their social level. As you can imagine, the gospel message of oneness in Christ cut right to the heart of this Roman value. The equal value of each believer in Christ was utterly foreign to the Roman system.

Another Roman social value was that of competition for honor, especially among free males. Seeking honor was a zero-sum game, for there was only so much to go around, and one inevitably had more while another had less. Every slight must be met with a comeback. And every gift must outdo the last. Even close friends competed between themselves for honor. Here is a modern example: in the musical Hamilton, both Hamilton and his son die in separate duels. These duels were the result of one man challenging another man's honor.

Both Roman values—social worth and social honor—are in play as Demetrius challenges Paul. Demetrius upholds the *pax Romana* as a good citizen should and expects Paul to defend his honor when challenged. Paul's instinct as a Roman citizen, familiar with urban settings from his birth, is to address the crowd. In other words, to rise to the challenge.

However, in an amazing show of humility, he listens to his friends and backs away. This is incredibly counter cultural or, said another way, an incredibly gospel-shaped response, speaking truth in love. Paul's friends have been taught well by their teacher. They see no need for Paul to show he is "right" and Demetrius is wrong. They see no need for Paul's honor to be defended in this way or to take honor from Demetrius. The truth of the gospel does not harm its opponents in the public shaming way nor does it give space for self-indulgent pride. Speaking the truth in love does not mean speaking up to defend one's personal honor or to "be right" when it hurts another or plays into the world's expectations about being right. Truth is never enough; it must be filled with Christ's love.

Third, speaking the truth in love is not only about how we engage with our opponents, but also how we serve others. To set the stage, let's remind ourselves of Paul's claims in Ephesians. He insists that the cross creates one new humanity, Jew and gentile, former enemies, now together as the temple of the Lord, as the body of Christ. Let's assume that they did what Paul asked in his epistle, namely that they were governed by their filling of the Holy Spirit: they gave thanks, they submitted to each other out of reverence for Christ, and they had a fellowship of co-heirs together, no hostility between Jew and gentile. What if, in other words, they practiced genuine love of those who were as unlike them as one could be? It makes sense of Revelation 2 that the first generation of believers in Ephesus did embrace Paul's vision and served each other with fervent love. They understood that Christ intended with his work on the cross to make a new humanity.

What if the second generation of believers in Ephesus forgot that the point of the cross was to make all things new? That Christ made peace, a peace that addressed their identity? This new identity made them part of something that earlier they would have had no interest in, namely a group that included "others." For Jews, that meant fellowship with gentiles, those "unclean" or "superstitious" or "barbarian" or "heathen"; for gentiles, it meant that odd minority group that did not honor the gods. In Christ, they are all now one body. This new humanity is not an erasure of the old identities, but a recalibration of their importance, such that the "other" is now valued above the "self."

Let me dig into this a bit more. In Paul's day, the owner or master would assume that she or he had more social worth than a slave. It was on this basis that the domination of the slave made sense. But in the church, the owner is not worth more, for Paul clearly says that God shows no favoritism to slave owners. And we can extend this to those outside the church, that God shows no favoritism towards any group or individual, but all are recipients of his prevenient grace. And all are welcome to receive God's great gift of salvation. Every person bears the image of his or her Creator.

Dr. Myrto Theocharous realized this truth in a new way as she worked with refugees and women caught in the sex slavery racket. She wanted to help those vulnerable people, and she tried to motivate other believers to help by pointing out that these powerless people also carried the image of God. Then she realized that the Bible did not draw out the logic that way. Instead, Scripture assumed the social worth, the *imago Dei* of each of these vulnerable. What was questioned was whether those in charge were living into their *imago Dei* status. Did those who have wealth give generously? If not, were they really imaging God? "I have realized that it is actually arrogant to serve the disadvantaged only in order to solve *their* problem. It is arrogant to serve them so that they can be 'human' just like I am. I am the one who is not human without them."[2] This is a profound recasting of the situation, and I wonder if this is what the Ephesus church of Revelation 2 needed. They forgot their first love, the love of God and neighbor. They saw the "truth" that they should work to feed the hungry, care for the sick, stand fast against idolatry. But they did so not because their very identity as one new humanity was at stake. They assumed that they were fine, and others needed them. Yet they lacked the one thing that held the gospel truth together: love. It is possible that the Ephesians abandoned their first love by forgetting their shared humanity, both as the body of Christ, and as sharing the image of God with all humanity.

There is a third possibility, not mutually exclusive with the other two, namely that the Ephesians placed themselves as their first love and became enthusiastic for their own social prestige, influence, and power within their group. While the earliest believers openly confessed their allegiance to Jesus and each other, publicly embraced shame, and repented of their previous use of magic, perhaps the second generation was less willing to admit sins, more focused on love of self (which is not the same as self-care) and self-promotion.

2. Theocharous, "Image of God and Justice," 49.

The attraction for personal glory and influence is not relegated to past ages. Even before social media, societies had their celebrities. One man who faced such a challenge was Eric Liddell, whose story is told in the 1981 movie *Chariots of Fire*.[3] Liddell's gold medal in the 400 meters at the 1924 Summer Olympics secured for him international fame. And his convictions about not competing on Sunday, thus missing the 100-meter race in which he was favored to win, reinforced in the public's mind his faith as a Christian. His victory in the 400 meters could be seen as God blessing him for his refusal to race on Sunday. We often go further to assume God will reward us publicly. I suggest that this belief is strongly held today by many in the churches.[4] It sounds something like this: God wants you to be successful and will reward your obedience and faithfulness with success in the human sphere.

Such logic was certainly in play in Liddell's time. We know that he was invited or encouraged to train for the 1932 Olympics. Dr. William Toop, a child when Liddell served in China, recalls the visit in 1929 to Tientsin, China, by Otto Peltzer, a celebrated German track star who broke four world records in 1926. On the outskirts of town at the edge of the British Concession was built a large recreation facility called Min Yuon or the People's Field. Liddell helped to design it. It was here that the two men raced, and Otto won his event, the 800 meter, while Eric won the 400 meter. The German insisted that the Scotsman return to the UK and train for the 1932 Olympics, but as Toop puts it, "Eric's diary had no room for that."[5] Yet the defeat in the 800 did not sit well with Liddell; he trained in China and eventually bested Peltzer's record. Clearly Liddell loved to run and still had a strong heart for competition. Moreover, he was capable of training for the Olympics and proved that he could potentially win events. But he believed that God had put other things before training for Olympics.

If he were alive today, I think he would be pulled very strongly into a preaching circuit. Auditoriums would fill to hear the man whom God blessed with material goods for his faithfulness. In fact, while he was in college, Liddell had a powerful preaching ministry. In 1923, the Rev. Dr. D. P. Thomson, who worked for the Glasgow Students' Evangelistic Union,

3. For general information, see Thomson, *Eric H. Liddell*.

4. The following three paragraphs on Eric Liddell are used by permission from Penn State University Press, Lynn H. Cohick, "Citizenship and Empire: Paul's Letter to the Philippians and Eric Liddell's Work in China," *JSPL* 1 (2011) 14–16. https://doi.org/10.2307/26426484.

5. Toop, "Recollections of Eric Liddell."

asked Eric to speak to a meeting of young men. He agreed and later told Thomson this was the turning point in his life[6] because it was the first time that he publicly owned and presented his faith. He continued to speak to enthusiastic crowds, and two hundred men took up the call to Christian ministry, and many people were persuaded to become missionaries based on his sermons.[7] This success and his natural teaching abilities, confirmed in the Anglo-Chinese school in Tientsin, led some of his close friends to counsel him against accepting a post in rural ministry.[8] But he apparently was less impressed with himself than they were. In its subtle forms, in a soft hero worship sort of way, the church loves its champions.

Eric Liddell was clear that his primary battle, if you will, was his own rebellious will to disobey. Said more positively, Liddell declares that the "key to knowing God, to having his peace and assurance in your heart . . . is obedience."[9] Such obedience comes as one submits to God's will. The promises of God are not that earthly honor follows sacrificial obedience, but that obedience deepens the well of joy and peace against which no human accolades, no Olympic gold medal, no crown of laurels compare. Liddell's final words are reported to be: "it's absolute surrender." Perhaps he was also thinking of Paul's words to Timothy, "I have fought the good fight, I have finished the race, I have kept the faith. Now there is in store for me the crown of righteousness."

In Eph 3:7–11, Paul describes himself as a servant of the gospel who is undeserving of such responsibility as was laid upon him to preach to the gentiles. The goal was not to preach to as many as he could; instead, it was to embolden the church to bear witness before the powers and principalities of this age to the grace of Christ that united Jew and gentile, slave and free, male and female. He changed the definition of victory from a numbers game, a results focus, to a call to obedience.

Paul asks Timothy and the church to pray for everyone, which would include the silversmiths. And to pray as one who has been shown mercy. Additionally, believers are to live peaceful lives. Recall that Christ is our peace, so this peace has tremendous creative power—it destroys enmity and creates a new, holy people. God desires that all come to know Christ and his wonderful, powerful love.

6. Thomson, *Eric H. Liddell*, 37.

7. Thomson, *Eric H. Liddell*, 40.

8. Thomson, *Eric H. Liddell*, 217.

9. Liddell, *Disciplines of the Christian Life*, 5.

In conclusion, Paul did not need to face down the hostile crowd in Ephesus. He did not need to "win" the argument with Demetrius. He did not play the Roman game of honor/shame. He spoke the truth and acted in love. He kept his focus on the kingdom of Christ and of God. Dr. Theocharous realized that love must infuse truth in a personal way. The truth is that all bear God's image, and enacting this must include attention to whether those with influence express godly love. As Eric Liddell's life expresses, this godly love does not seek self-acclamation, even if it leads to souls saved, for God-like love is self-sacrificial love that seeks the welfare of others. The Ephesian church needed to be rooted and established in this love, and the call rings out to us today.

Ephesians 4:17–32: Put on the New Self in Christ

Throughout Ephesians, Paul draws a sharp contrast between the ways of the world and the way of Christ. At the beginning of this chapter, Paul asks that the Ephesians walk in the truth of their oneness. Paul stresses the one God equipping the church for growth to maturity and for the works of service (see "good works" in Eph 2:10). In the second half of the chapter, Paul repeats his call to walk well, this time mindful of their new self in Christ. We will see in chapter 5 that Paul continues his emphasis on walking rightly, as Paul contrasts the pagan way of life, one filled with darkness, and walking in Christ's light. Overall, in chapter 4 Paul emphasizes the holy lifestyle as essential because it is rooted in two key theological truths. First, the God who calls believers is the one God; therefore, believers have unity in the Lord and the Spirit and must exhibit this oneness in their community life. Second, Christ has supplied the full measure of grace for the church to grow to maturity, with a gift that provides ways for the truth of the gospel to be understood, lived out, and passed down through the church's life. Although this chapter is filled with ethical demands, these are not arbitrary lists related to hollow legalism but reflect the very character of God. And although this chapter stresses key theological teachings, Paul does not imagine that correct doctrine is sufficient without active demonstrations of it, for "knowledge puffs up, but love builds up" (1 Cor 8:1 NIV 2011).

This passage contrasts the typical gentile religious mindset with that of a believer whose mind is renewed in Christ and whose actions reflect this identity. Paul imagines believers wearing Christ, putting on Christ, having previously taken off their old, pagan worldview. Paul focuses on the ignorance and futility of the pagan mindset, in contrast to the truth and holiness that characterize believers. The mindset shift results in truth-telling, in generosity, in wholesome speech and honest labor. The new self demonstrates forgiveness, and resists grumbling, slander, and anger.

Ephesians 4:17–24

Paul spends three verses, a single sentence, warning believers not to fall back into their previous ways of thinking (4:17–19). Recall that at the beginning of chapter 2, Paul indicated that gentiles walk under the influence of the prince of this age and are thus disobedient to God. Paul then painted a picture of gentiles walking from far away to come close to God, in Christ. The gentile was outside the family of God, outside his promises and community, but now was a family member in the house of God. In our passage, Paul does not focus on sin, or on kinship, but on worldview. He emphasizes the futility of this darkened mindset, an emptiness that lacks purpose and leads to regret.

As we explore the passage, I should note at the outset that Paul does not ask the gentile believer to become a Jew, that is, to become a proselyte. The gentile did not need to take up kosher food laws or circumcision or commit to Sabbath rest or make pilgrimages to Jerusalem or keep new moon festivals or Passover. They could continue to eat their traditional foods, marry within their language and people group, and work in their shops. What they needed to change was their worldview, to bring it in line with the redemption of God in Christ. This was a heavy lift, for it meant rethinking life goals, the definition of success and happiness, and the content of truth. This meant pulling back from the worship of Artemis of the Ephesians and the pride that went along with being in her city, Ephesus. This meant rejecting the imperial claims of Rome, which promoted a highly stratified culture that made social self-worth the measure of all happiness.

I should also note that Jews who esteemed Jesus as Messiah also had changes to make in their mindset, but their changes were different to those required of the gentile converts. One might say that Jews, such as Paul, worshiped the true God, but now that the messiah Jesus has come, Jews who worship God rightly or fully must also believe in Jesus as messiah. Paul did not need to "convert" from a pagan mindset, but he did acknowledge that the sinful world impacted him towards impiety and sin (2:3). The big issue for Paul and other Jews was not God's identity as holy but understanding that God's people are now made holy because of Christ and the Holy Spirit. God's people do not hold in common a celebration of Sabbath or refusing to eat pork. God's people share in the Holy Spirit and enjoy salvation "in Christ" who makes believers holy, clean, and pure. Thus, he reminds all believers that they are "members of one body" (4:25).

In 4:17, Paul repeats the verb "to walk" from 4:1, here warning gentile believers not to walk as they once had walked, living in a world of ignorance and darkness. Paul speaks against their deeds of sensuality (4:19), which includes socially unacceptable actions and a lack of self-restraint, as well as sexual immorality. Paul also points to greed (4:18; 5:3). We will focus more specifically on greed in the next section. In our passage, this darkened mindset, with its attending behaviors, cannot see the light or the Son. The self has replaced God at the center of life. Such a worldview is outside the "life of God" (4:18), an interesting phrase used by Paul to speak of life in its fullest, most purposeful, and fulfilled sense. This phrase captures Paul's bedrock conviction that believers are in Christ.

This ignorance is not morally neutral, for it leads to a hardening of the heart and then actions of greed and impurity. As the heart hardens, the mind grows ever more callous and desensitized to the beauty and goodness of God, his creation, and his people. The underbelly of such callousness is despair. This dire situation, however, does not absolve the gentile of responsibility for actions done in ignorance and darkness. Paul expects gentiles to be self-aware enough to ponder the universe and to know themselves and pursue truth about God. Paul also indicates that gentiles made the decision to give themselves over to this futility, with its enticements of wealth and sensual pleasures (see also Rom 1:24–28). The behavior is habitual, with the pitiless downward spiral of darkened mindset producing self-centered, immoral behavior, which hardens the heart, leading to more darkness and additional sin and futility. And this behavior harms others; greed takes from neighbors, and sexual excesses are gratified by slaves or those of lower social status. Paul does not excuse such behavior on account of the perpetrator's ignorance of God.

Paul paints a bleak picture of the gentile's religious life outside of God's redemptive plan in Christ. This is an abstract, high-level description, not a detailed, granular account of each unbeliever's life. We have all met nice, kind, caring unbelievers (and mean, spiteful, nasty believers). Paul emphasizes the futility of paganism as it pulls people from God's life and into despair. The sinful behaviors in which the gentile believers formerly indulged are a pathway to utter futility and emptiness. But Paul has a better way.

The next sentence (in Greek) includes four verses (4:20–24) that offer hope and promise that believers can live in newness of life. Paul has every expectation that the Ephesians are made new in Christ, and this passage reiterates this reality. Several expressions, however, are a bit unusual and deserve a closer look.

First, Paul speaks of the Ephesians as having "learned" Christ (4:20). He does not say "learned about" Christ, a more natural expression, since we think of learning about a thing. Paul speaks of wanting to know Christ, and we often use "know" when referring to a person (Phil 3:10). He continues in this vein, declaring that the Ephesians "heard" Christ, although some English translations soften this abruptness by adding the preposition "about." Finally, Paul indicates that the believers were taught "in him." We would expect Paul to say that they were taught Christ, but again the syntax is unusual. Most likely, Paul modifies the expected syntax both to emphasize the relationship believers have in and with Christ and to underline the title "Christ" or Messiah.

Captured in the title "Christ" are the promises and predictions of the Old Testament. The Messiah brings peace (2:14), drawing together Jew and gentile as foretold by prophets as they glimpsed God's redemptive plan (2:17). Moreover, the Messiah is over all spiritual forces (1:20–21) and resides in each believer (3:16–17). The Messiah has his church, his body, and a temple made up of his followers (2:22). And this Messiah has a name: Jesus. Paul rarely uses the name Jesus without his title "Christ." The context here suggests that Paul wants the Ephesians to recall the historical Jesus's life, ministry, death, and bodily resurrection (Rom 8:11; Gal 6:17; Phil 2:10).

Second, Paul transforms a male rite of passage to be representative of a believer's new faith. Paul describes believers taking off their old self (*anthropos*) and putting on their new self (see also Col 3:9–10). These images would call to mind the Roman ceremony of a young man putting on a toga for the first time. The *toga virilis* ritual was not about clothing *per se*, but about the youth's entrance to adulthood. The toga symbolized authority and maturity, and it came with the expectation that the "new" man would behave with wisdom and self-control. Paul draws on the image of putting on something that changes one's status in the community, but his new *anthropos* does not look like an ideal Roman man, but as the crucified and risen Lord Jesus Christ.

Paul connects taking off old clothes and putting on new clothes with baptism in Romans (Rom 6:2–8; see also Gal 3:27; Col 2:11–12). Paul discusses baptism in the context of continuing to act in ways that reflect disobedience towards God's holy expectations. It is important to remember that Paul desired to live a righteous life, for that was the way of joy, love, and peace. To the metaphor of unclothing and clothing, Paul adds dying and rising, for in baptism, the believer dies in Christ and is raised to new life. Death was necessary because that is the doorway out of this world; it is the key that unlocks the handcuffs by which the ruler of this world has kept humanity captive.

While it is the case that Paul mentions "one baptism" in 4:5, he does not focus on this topic in the remainder of the chapter. Therefore, it is less likely that Paul wants his listeners/readers to recall the rite of baptism here. Instead, Paul connects the "putting off" and "putting on" and his call to "be made new" back to the main verb "to learn." Paul emphasizes the accomplished fact that believers have removed their old self and put on a new self when they embraced the gospel. Most likely, Paul stresses the completeness of their new life in Christ and not so much that this happened in the past. Included in the clothing imagery is an important note about renewing the mind. The point is that the new self has a new outlook. If I could draw an analogy, the renewing of the mind is like me putting on my reading glasses to see the print. It is a daily task that allows me to see clearly. So too, believers are to daily renew their attitudes and see things as God in Christ sees the world. With proper clothing and glasses, the believer is prepared to live like Christ.

Paul declares that this new self is directly connected with the truth summed up in Jesus. It is unusual for Paul to use the name Jesus without his title, Christ. Perhaps Paul is calling to the readers' minds the historical ministry of Jesus, and his incarnation, passion, and resurrection. Paul points to a person, not an ideology or theory. Paul declares that the Ephesian believers learned Christ, and the Greek does not include "about." Learning a person suggests intimacy and friendship, whereas learning "about" someone can remain at a detached level, objectifying that person. Paul stresses that believers' behavior is tied to the savior's behavior; believers' identity is tied to the savior's redemption.

Third, Paul highlights that the new self is created by God, and it is to live out the holiness and righteousness that characterizes God. At first glance, this is an audacious statement, for what human can be like God? But Paul likely has in mind the Genesis account which indicates that humans, male and female, are made in God's image (*eikon*). This idea of being transformed into Christ's likeness is not new in Paul's letters (Rom 8:29; 2 Cor 3:18; Col 3:10). All this is the work of God in believers' lives, it is not through human effort that one achieves this holiness (2:10). God's holiness is not reflected in a "holier than thou" attitude, but in prioritizing the things that matter to God. It includes avoiding sin and pursuing goodness, kindness, and joy. Again, God's righteousness is not simply morality, and especially not virtue signaling (the curse of social media), but God's righteousness includes expressions of justice and mercy. Both virtues are public, community-focused, and intended to benefit others. Paul ends his sentence with the phrase "of truth." With this, Paul reminds readers of his description in 4:21, that Jesus is truth, that the gospel message is the true message of God's redemption. Believers are made new in Jesus Christ, who is the way, the truth, and the life (John 14:6).

Ephesians 4:25–32

The remaining verses in this chapter provide specific examples of what the new self should look like, and it has nothing to do with viewing oneself in a mirror. Quite the opposite, for Paul indicates that we "see" our new self as we interact with others, especially (but not only) those in the church body. Paul commands that believers speak truth to each other, resist the satisfying feeling of self-serving anger against another or gossiping. Believers obey these commands in community.

Paul commands that believers speak truthfully (4:25) because this behavior reflects the person who is the way, the truth, and the life (John 14:6; Eph 4:21). The phrase "speak truthfully to your neighbor" is closely related to Zech 8:16 in the Greek text. The context of the Old Testament passage is God's restoration of Israel in Jerusalem, where planting and harvesting will be done in peace. God commands that the faithful who enjoy such blessing speak truth to each other and make just judgements. He gives orders against false oaths and evil plans. Paul understands the hand-in-glove connection between truth-telling and truthful actions, for both are necessary to show the life of Christ in each believer who has put on Christ. The following exhortations, therefore, are not merely practical advice, nor should each injunction be seen as a nice moral aphorism. Instead, we should read these several verses as an integrated fabric of the life lived truthfully before the one who is Truth. The morality espoused by Paul is useful in general for a well-functioning community, but that is not why he urges truth-telling in its various forms. Paul desires that believers reflect God's likeness more and more, his righteousness and holiness, extending forgiveness to others (4:24; 5:1).

Paul enjoins believers in specific behaviors that help grow truth-telling and truthful living, coordinating head, heart, and hands in a life of truth before Jesus. In this section, a pattern emerges of a negative command, followed by a positive command with an explanation as to its purpose. Paul commands that believers cease their stealing. The deeds Paul likely has in mind are cheating customers or failing to return what is owned or using unjust scales in weighing out food. The stealing relates to unjust business practices or taking advantage of one's neighbors. The antidote for the desire to steal is to imagine giving of one's labor to help others. Stealing privileges the self (Paul is not thinking of the mother who "steals" bread for her children) while work done rightly provides for the community. In a well-functioning community, a mother would have bread for her children.

Paul wants the Ephesians to use their speech wisely, which includes avoiding bitterness or slander (4:31). It means refraining from speech when tempers flare and apologizing when unkind and heated words were spoken. Paul cites Ps 4:4 in verse 4:26 in his concern about anger (see also 4:31 for the cognate noun). The verse commands anger, and most interpreters think the command is conditioned on the following negative command to not sin. However, it is more likely that Paul commands a certain type of anger, the anger against injustice and sin. This sort of anger should lead to actions that right the wrongs or shuts down the sin. But there is another sort of anger that believers must resist, that of self-righteous pique or outrage. This second sort of anger can be rationalized as the former, but it is driven by pride and resentment (see also Jas 3:6–10; 4:11–12). It is not always easy to discern the motifs of our hearts, and the story of Cain and Abel instructs us that sin is always waiting to pounce (Gen 4:5–7). Anger must not fester, for it destroys a community or relationship. Paul offers the poetic line that one should not let the sun go down on one's anger. But there might be more than poetry to this, for the Jewish day is calculated to begin at nightfall.

Thus, at sunset, a new day starts, a new day that should not be encumbered with the anger of the previous day.

Paul wraps up his discussion of the new self by reminding the Ephesians of their own forgiven, redeemed status in the Lord. Paul summarizes his call to action by commanding them to be kind and compassionate, the latter term is found only here in Paul, and in 1 Pet 3:8. The reference for what kind and compassionate look like is found at the end of the sentence, namely God the Father and the Son, Jesus Christ. If we want to know what kindness looks like, think about Christ's actions. If we want to understand compassion, think about the adoption into God's family established by the Father, who blesses believers with all blessings in Christ (1:3–6). The next verse, Eph 5:1, commands that believers imitate God. What an awesome and terrifying thought. We will turn to that breathtaking thought in our next chapter, but we should not forget Eph 4:32, wherein Paul stresses the forgiveness that believers received, and are to extend to others, because God forgave in Christ.

Ephesians 4:17–32: Reflections for Preaching and Teaching

The central theme of this passage is an example of the two ways tradition that flows through Scripture. In sum, there are two paths human can choose: life or death, obedience to God or sin. Moses offers this in his charge that the Israelites must choose between following God, which brings life, or pursuing idols, which leads to destruction (Deut 30:11–18). It is not enough to acknowledge that God is one (over against paganism), for even the demons know as much and tremble (Jas 2:19). It is not enough to say you love God if you hate your fellow believers (1 John 1: 9; 4:19–21). Salvation is not merely agreeing with theological propositions, as important as those are, but must include modeling Christ. Discard the old self that was greedy, selfish, and heartless, and start acting as one who has been made new by Jesus Christ. Start living the reality of who you are.

As I reflected on the importance of community in establishing one's new self, I thought of the cartoon, *Peanuts* by Charles Schultz, where Linus shouts, "I love humanity, it's people I can't stand!" The sentiment goes back to *The Brothers Karamazov*, from a scene where a wealthy woman sees a group of peasants gathered around an elder, and she remarks that she loves the people too. She doubts that she has faith, and the elder says that you could convince yourself that you have it if you demonstrate love to your neighbor, for then you will know the reality of God more clearly. The elder told a story of a man who said, "I love humanity, but I wonder at myself. The more I love humanity in general, the less I love man in particular." He continued that he imagines great deeds he would do for humanity, but he gets impatient with living with another for even two days. "As soon as anyone is near me, his personality disturbs my self-complacency and restricts my freedom. In twenty-four hours I begin to hate the best of men: one because he's too long over his dinner; another because he has a cold and keeps on blowing his nose."[10] The elder continues his conversation with the wealthy woman, explaining much as Paul does to the Ephesians that love in action is hard, long, and often done in the shadows. Cheap love, as that which loves "humanity," is greedy, self-serving, a performance that desires the limelight.

Paul had personal experience with destructive dynamics, in Corinth. Paul relates that a believer had slandered him publicly, and he requested that the church firmly address the situation. The man apologized, repented, and Paul encouraged the community to welcome him back, for the alternative of hanging on to anger would destroy the church (2 Cor 2:5–11). A work culture or church culture is not always easy to discern, but we should not underestimate the power of culture.[11] Culture gives the members of the group their sense of identity, their sense of what is valuable and the behaviors that are rewarded. A toxic environment disempowers its members while valuing productivity and performance that does not allow for rest and renewal. The leadership exhibits narcissistic qualities, which include an inflated sense of self, a need for others to acknowledge their superiority, coupled with a lack of empathy and a sensitivity to criticism. Authority and power are shown by creating fear and intimidation. People matter less than the institution, and loyalty to that institution matters more than doing the right thing.

The qualities of the new self, created after God's own character, challenge and correct the characteristics of a toxic environment. Paul asks that believers encourage each other, build up and not disempower. Believers speak the truth, not harshly, but with compassion. Believers are productive not because they seek material growth or gain, but so that they might share with others (4:28). Paul urges forgiveness, which implies that people and institutions can do wrong things. Hiding sins creates a festering mess. Paul

10. Dostoevsky, *Brothers Karamazov*, book 2, chapter 4.
11. McKnight and Barringer, *Church Called Tov*; McKnight and Barringer, *Pivot*.

denounces rage and malice as grieving the Holy Spirit, a direct challenge to the narcissistic leader who creates fear and rejects well-meaning criticism.

Paul knows that allowing gossip and grumbling, believing the worst about the other, divides and conquers the body of Christ (4:27; see also Ps 101:5). Often, we hide our gossip under the label of "prayer requests." We rationalize that by listening to another's complaints, we're only offering a shoulder to cry on; however, allowing the complainant to slander another's reputation in the name of lending a compassionate ear was not acceptable in Corinth in Paul's day and should not be tolerated in Christian circles today (see also Num 12:1–15; 16:1–35).

EPHESIANS 5

Ephesians 5:1–17: Live as Beloved Children of Light

CHAPTER 5 CONTINUES THE injunctions of the previous chapter, but with a greater emphasis on several metaphors of opposites (idolatry/fidelity; darkness/light; fruitlessness/fruitfulness; unwise/wise). Paul adds three additional topics, sexual immorality, impurity, greed, and frames his argument in terms of a believer's eternal inheritance in Christ. Paul's main hope is that the promised kingdom of Christ and of God (5:5) will inspire believers to follow God's example and Christ's self-sacrificial love. The foundation on which such inspiration stands is the believer's own membership as beloved children in God's family through Christ. We must not read this section of Scripture as a list of dos and don'ts, for that removes the narrative context in which Paul sets this teaching. It is because the believer is already a member of God's family, already clothed with Christ, already seated with him, already established as an heir, that these behaviors have any eternal value. The behaviors don't secure salvation or earn salvation points; instead, they foster the goodness and peace that is already present through Christ and the Holy Spirit in the midst of the church.

Ephesians 5:1–2

Verses 1–2 serve as a transition from the previous verse, in that the verb "to be" or "to become" is found in both. Ephesians 5:1 reads literally "be imitators of God." The connection between 4:32 and 5:1 is important because it provides context for the command to imitate God. Most likely, Paul refers here to imitating God's forgiving character, shown most clearly in the forgiveness of sins enjoyed through faith in Christ's work on the cross. We could go a bit broader here to say believers can imitate God's generosity in showing compassion and kindness, mercy and love (2:4; 4:32). Elsewhere Paul speaks of imitating his walk as he imitates Christ (1 Cor 4:16; 11:1; Phil 3:17; 1 Thess 1:16), and he encourages believers to imitate those in their midst who are worthy of such (1 Thess 2:14). We are not called to imitate the incarnation, for that is a singular event unique to the divine-human Christ.[1] The Son is the preexistent second person of the Trinity, transcendent and separate from his creation. Jesus the Messiah did not come from another culture (a culture of heaven) then learn another culture (Jewish) and identify with it to witness to it. He was fully human, with his own particularity—a first-century Jewish male. Instead, believers imitate Christ's obedience, even to death on the cross (Phil 2:8). Believers are united with Christ, a member of his body (1:22–23), and are invited to take up their own crosses (Luke 9:23–24; Gal 2:20). It is not the incarnation but the suffering that believers imitate in their union with Christ (Phil 3:10; Col 1:24).

Paul starts 5:1 with "therefore" and will continue his focus on walking in love, as Christ walks, using the verb "to walk" (sometimes translated as "to live") in several verses (5:2, 8, 15). We also find repeated in the section addressing husbands later in the chapter a call for them to love their wives with the self-sacrificial love Christ expressed on the cross. This offering is singular, and all-sufficient, so that no human (husbands included) need add anything to its effective work nor can be responsible for another's spiritual maturity. Christ's sacrifice was a voluntary demonstration of his love, part of the redemption plan established by the Trinity before the foundation of the world (1:4–8).

Ephesians 5:3–6

It is as beloved children of the Father, united with Christ and seated with him in the heavenly places, that believers are able to act in ways that reflect their "family" background. The three sins referred to, sexual immorality (*porneia*), impurity, and greed, cut to the heart of humanity's alienation from God, while the call for holiness in 5:3–8 stresses acting with goodness towards others. Paul lived in a world where free men had multiple ways to access sex. Men had sexual partners in addition to their wives. Prostitutes, male and female, were plentiful and inexpensive, and there was no moral shame attached to men having sex with them. The sexual availability of

1. Billings, *Union with Christ*, 124–45.

slaves, male and female, boys and girls, was ubiquitous. Sex was transactional, objectifying, and could be sadistic.[2] Paul's injunction against sexual immorality protected the vulnerable.[3] (Not that Paul's instructions were unique to Christ-followers. Jewish moral codes, expressed in the Scriptures, decried adultery, prostitution, and sex with slaves. Paul reflected such beliefs to the Ephesians.)

Impurity is an unfamiliar word to many today but would have conjured up ideas of sacred space and human purity necessary to enter it. Such purity could be focused on the physical, such as menstrual purity codes within Judaism or prohibitions against those who did not wash before entering a temple shrine. Such behavior was not only an individual's infraction, but also it threatened the community if such behavior angered the gods. The term here likely connotes a *moral* uncleanness. Paul used the word earlier in 4:19 when speaking about gentiles' futile lives that sear their consciences and harden their hearts; they indulge their sensual passions. The same idea holds here.

The third sin is that of greed, which might include the sense of greedily fulfilling one's lusts. Yet more likely Paul shifts focus, for this noun is not connected with "and" as were sexual immorality and impurity. Greed is something easily seen in others but rarely viewed in oneself. Perhaps we rationalize that we *really* need this money or item now or might need it in the future. We think (but usually don't say aloud) that we deserve the money, thing, status, or position. When we see greed in others, it is usually because we sense our own lack or loss, or that of another individual or community. Greed takes much and leaves little. While we all admit that greed is bad, even very bad, we might feel that Paul is too harsh to say that "greed is idolatry" as Paul does in our passage (5:5; Col 3:5; see also 1 Thess 4:6–7). This deserves a closer look.

Paul indicates that the sexually immoral or greedy person will not share an inheritance in the kingdom of Christ and of God (5:5). Three key teachings emerge from this passage (5:4–7). First, Paul speaks about not inheriting the kingdom because of sexual immorality and greed in two other letters. In 1 Corinthians, Paul addresses the civil cases one believer brings against another, likely about failure to repay debt. Paul lists the greedy as one group who will not inherit (1 Cor 6:9–10), probably pointing the finger

2. The classicist, Sarah Ruden, *Paul Among the People*, 3–118, offers a view of Paul from an ancient Greek and a Greco-Roman backdrop.

3. Harper, *From Shame to Sin*, 19–79.

at the one who brings the lawsuit. In this case, a wealthier believer pulls the poor believer into court, a setting notoriously corrupt and tilted towards the wealthy. To demand repayment would mean deeper poverty for the fellow believer. Paul acknowledges that payment is legally required in his response: Why not rather be wronged? He challenges the believer to give up the right to repayment, for the sake of the fellow believer's well-being, and to protect the loaner from falling into greed. In Gal 5:18–21, which mentions only idolatry, not greed, in its long list of sins, Paul likewise warns that those who habitually act in such ways have no share in the kingdom. Remember, Paul's concern is the vulnerable, those sexually objectified, and those impoverished through the greed of others. These actions grieve the Holy Spirit and destroy community.

Second, Paul insists to the Ephesians (and to the Corinthians and Galatians) that he is confident that they do not belong in the camp of the disobedient. They will inherit the kingdom of Christ and of God. Paul indicates that they are sealed with the Holy Spirit (1:13), that they are alive with Christ (2:5), and, a few verses earlier, that they are beloved children (5:1). The warnings serve to distinguish the behaviors of those clothed with Christ, having put on the new self, and those who have not. Even more, perhaps, the warnings paint a picture of the selfish, amoral disregard for others from which sexual immorality, impurity, and greed arise. This is not how you learned Christ (4:20).

The mention of Christ in reference to the kingdom of God is unique to Ephesians and probably relates to his insistence that Christ is seated at God's right hand (1:20–22; 2:6). For Paul, the kingdom is both future and here now. We see its temporal expression in Paul's insistence that Christ has defeated sin and death and in his comments to the Romans that the kingdom of God is not a matter of eating (kosher or non-kosher) but of righteousness, peace, and joy in the Holy Spirit (Rom 14:17; for a negative example, see 1 Cor 4:20). And Paul points to its future when he reminds the Philippians that they are citizens of heaven, a separate kingdom ruled by Christ the savior, who will return and transform into his likeness all the faithful (Phil 3:20–21).

Ephesians 5:7–17

Paul warns not only against doing evil deeds, but also partnering or partaking with those who do (5:7, 11, 16). Paul recognizes the frailty of human will and the strong pull of sinful pleasures. He says much the same thing when urging believers to put on the armor of God (6:11–13; see also 4:27), that they stand fast, not attack the powers of the dark world. So too Peter warns against the devil, as one who stalks the unwary believer, and calls believers to resist him (1 Pet 5:8–9). Likewise, James urges believers to resist (Jas 4:7). Both Peter and James use the same verb translated as "withstand" in Eph 6:13. Scripture does not underestimate the devil's power, nor overestimate human capacity to do battle. Moreover, the apostles' warning presumed that Christians would resist together, as a community supporting each other.

With a show of psychological brilliance, Paul does not speak only of what to avoid, but of what to emulate. Believers are light in the Lord; thus, they can live in the light (Col 1:12–14). The light allows good works of truth and justice and opens the door to further understanding of what God's will is. And as more believers demonstrate more truth and justice, and light shines more brightly, darkness has nowhere to go. Not because darkness itself was targeted, but because light took up more space. Wisdom was heeded with greater frequency, and foolishness had less airtime. As believers get more comfortable in the light, their knowledge of God's will becomes clearer and deeper. And as the light is brighter, sleepers wake up (5:14), likely a reference to unbelievers accepting the gospel truth.

The call to holiness that Paul presents in these verses is a call to joy-filled living. It is a picture of seeing where you are going (5:8), having purpose in your work (fruit, 5:9), and understanding God better (5:10, 17). This is Paul's vision of growing into maturity in Christ (4:15).

Ephesians 5:1–17: Reflections for Preaching and Teaching

Paul gives three commands in this passage, reflecting his fundamental point that actions must match our confession. The believer must imitate God (5:1), walk in Christ's love (5:2), and be filled with the Holy Spirit (5:18). Christian discipleship is not about following rules but being in relationship with the triune God. Believers inherit (5:5), which implies that believers are in a family. Paul contrasts the holy life with one consumed with greed and sexual immorality, two human behaviors that continue to ruin lives and wreck families today.

Paul's discussion about sexual immorality in this section can sound harsh and judgmental to our ears, and these verses have been used to bludgeon women and children especially. But Paul speaks them to the community of equals, all beloved children, sharing a Father, with Jesus as their firstborn brother, through whom they share an inheritance. We don't need to hear a thunderous voice behind these words, but perhaps those of a gentle, wise elder who has seen much sin and wants his congregation to live in the light that is theirs through Christ.

What is Paul getting at when he writes that "greed is idolatry"? Perhaps the best way to understand the claim is as a metaphor, for then one can ask, "in what sense is greed like idolatry?"[4] Metaphor allows us to expand our understanding of idolatry beyond the physical image/idol of a god or goddess. The Old Testament offers several examples of this way of talking about idolatry. Scripture speaks of trusting, loving, worshiping, and serving only God. Idolatry puts something or someone in the place of God, gives honor and worship to something or someone other than God, and serves with passion something or someone other than God. Idolatry is habitual, a mindset, a worldview, or posture—not simply a set of individual sins against God from which we receive forgiveness upon repentance. Idolatry, as Paul uses it here in connection with greed, is a demeanor that privileges self over others and God.

Three historical examples of interpreting this teaching might help us today connect with the text's power and importance. From the second century, the Shepherd of Hermas includes an allegory of the church. In this vision, the seer, Hermas, is shown a tower being constructed with stones. The stones are of many sorts and are shaped to fit into the structure, which symbolizes the church. Some stones are round and white, and they are not being used in the building. The seer asks the Lady, who is leading him in his vision, why these are lying on the ground. She replies that they represent believers who have much wealth. When times of persecution arise, they deny the Lord to protect their money and businesses. Not until their shape is chiseled into blocks, that is, until their wealth is chipped away, will they be suitable for the tower. The Lady concludes that unless the rich have their wealth cut away, they cannot be useful for the Lord. She makes a personal comment to Hermas, that he was once wealthy, and was useless to God, but now he can be useful. In this case, clinging to wealth led to denying God, which, if not repented of, results in apostasy.

About two hundred years later, John Chrysostom, bishop of Constantinople (d. 407), spoke passionately on this passage in his 18th Homily on

---

4. Rosner, *Greed as Idolatry*, 47.

Ephesians. He emphasized that Paul was not referring to the physical act of bowing to an object/idol. Rather, Paul emphasized obedience, which is true worship. Chrysostom warns against the dangers of serving money, mammon, drawing on Jesus's teachings (Matt 6:24).

Martin Luther spoke extensively about greed as idolatry, explaining that greed shows a lack of trust in God, and thus is idolatry (*WA* 30,1:33–39). The greedy depend on their wealth, they hope in their money, they imagine that their things will bring them comfort. Luther draws on the first commandment, to love the Lord with all your heart, soul, and strength (Deut 6:1–13). He also points to the Lord's Prayer, specifically the request that God give us our daily bread (Matt 6:11; Luke 11:3), so that we are not tempted to grab for more (*WA* 19:96, 7–8).

In sum, we can think of greed as idolatry in several ways, including in terms of wealth accumulation making a believer useless to God, and as disobedient or disordered priorities with God in second place, or as placing hope or security in temporary things, not our eternal inheritance in God. The most important take-away is the seriousness of greed; it amounts to denying the one true God and often harming others. While the church tends to talk quite a lot (and not always faithfully) about sexual immorality, it seems not so concerned about the dangers of greed. Paul thinks otherwise.

Ephesians 5:18–33: Household Codes and Marriage

This section of Scripture depends on an understanding of ancient social customs of family structure and meals for its interpretation. The passage assumes a church meeting occurring in a home and including a meal, probably with communion. Thus, it is critical for readers today to understand what the earliest believers in Ephesus took for granted in Paul's message so that we can discern Paul's counter-cultural gospel claims. The first-century world inherited from classical Athens a hierarchically structured plan of the family, including husband/wife, father/children, and owner/slave. These three pairs made up the family, and if the elite families were well ordered, so too the city would be prosperous. I mention this now, and will elaborate below, because it is important to see that Paul was expected to treat these three categories if he wished to speak about the household. We need not conclude that Paul approved of this way of arranging society, indeed, I hope to show that he had serious concerns about its hierarchical use of power, and he taught that the gospel dismantled such destructive power.

One way he does this is by addressing the subordinate member of the pair first, wives, children, slaves. Most philosophers did not even address the subordinate member, but Paul honors them by addressing them first. Paul desires mutuality among the believers, based on their shared worship of God and their love of each other in the Lord. By focusing on Christ as the center of community, believers honor others above themselves and seek the welfare of all.

Ephesians 5:18–21

It may seem odd to begin the section on the household by talking about not drinking excessively, but such made perfect sense in Paul's world. In 5:18, Paul condemns getting drunk with wine and contrasts that with a command to be filled with the Holy Spirit. Before looking at that command, a word about meals at that time. Meals were a key venue where social status could be displayed and where honor and shame were in play. The Athenian elite men of the classical period, about four hundred years before Christ, held banquets followed by a symposium, a learned conversation. Yet not all such events were dignified, and not a few turned into a rowdy drinking party that included prostitutes. By the Roman period, men and their wives attended banquets, and these meals might include those of lower economic or social status. In the latter case, such meals might be sponsored by a trade guild or a funerary club or celebrate a wedding or birthday. In any case, the danger, from Paul's perspective, was excessive drinking that led to immoral behavior. We should not assume Paul has in mind here only sexual immorality. Banquet meals of the elite were notorious for wastefulness, an example of conspicuous consumption. In a time where food could be scarce, wasting it showed a disregard for the poor in the community. The Roman philosophers were not troubled by this lack of concern; however, they still cautioned against excess of any kind, as demonstrating self-control, a key virtue of the day. Often such admonition fell on deaf ears.

Paul, however, took seriously the charge to consider others at meals, as shown in 1 Corinthians. Paul critiques the church for failing to hold a true communion meal (1 Cor 11:17–34). Instead, each person eats what they brought, and indulges while others' stomachs growl. It does not matter that proper words are spoken over the bread and wine, for the actions of the wealthy in humiliating the poor make void any sense that this meal is holy (11:20–22). Paul charges them to see their actions as unworthy, as sinning against Christ himself, and against his body, which is the church. In asking for members to examine themselves, Paul is not advocating navel-gazing, or personal self-reflection on deeds done in the past week. He pleads with the members to look around, see the faces of their brothers and sisters, and make sure they share in the meal. Some of these gaunt faces are sick, even dying, due to malnourishment (11:30). This request to share food cuts to the heart of the Greco-Roman hierarchy system of self-worth, but it is the gospel reality.

To the Ephesians, Paul commands that they be filled with the Holy Spirit. Of course, they have been sealed with the Spirit, secure in their inheritance (1:13; 4:30). Paul commands that they live under the influence, so to speak, of the Spirit, in contrast to control of alcohol. Paul provides a description of what it looks like when the Holy Spirit animates their lives personally and their church collectively. He lists five participles (verbal adjective or verbs ending in "ing" in English) including: speaking, singing, making music, giving thanks, submitting. The English text divides this lengthy Greek sentence to create two or three shorter sentences, so it reads better. It is important, however, for readers to recognize the grammatical connection between the filling of the Holy Spirit and the worship of the Triune God, offering thanksgiving to God, and submission to the others in the congregation because of their reverence or awe of Christ.

Several points should be made about the participle "submit." First, while it is possible for participles to be translated as imperatives, it is not mandated. Paul used an imperative when he called believers to be filled with the Spirit, and he will use one again when he commands husbands to love their wives. In 5:20, "submitting" is a characteristic of a Spirit-filled believer, and this posture is demanding the same attitudes and actions as found at the beginning of chapter 4, that believers be humble, gentle, patient, loving (4:2), and kind and compassionate (4:32). Second, such submission is done to other members of the church, even as believers show gentleness and kindness to each other. This expectation is all-inclusive; slave owners are not exempt from submitting or being patient with their slaves, for example. Paul levels the social hierarchy of worth that pervaded his wider society, because of Christ.

Third, the phrase "reverence for Christ," occurs only here in the New Testament, and Paul's placement of it at the beginning of his household codes discussion alerts us to its importance. Reverence is not a term used frequently in casual speech today; its meaning is to express worship, adoration, veneration, to express devotion that is in awe or wonder at the object of worship. Paul repeats "reverence" or "awe/fear" in speaking of wives' response to their husbands (5:33), and slaves to their masters (6:5), thereby establishing the perimeters of submission. It is not submission based on society's declaration of one's self-worth. It is a believer's worship and adoration of Christ that inspires and empowers the giving of the self for the sake of others. The sort of submission Paul enjoins would certainly have felt uncomfortable, even demeaning, to some of those in the congregation, those who society said deserved to be honored. And it would have felt immensely affirming to those at the bottom of the social ladder, who had never received compassion.

Jesus spoke of such a situation in his parable about Lazarus and the rich man (Luke 16:19–31). The story describes the social blindness of a rich man, who never saw his fellow human being, Lazarus, begging at his gate. Even in death, the rich man felt he could order Lazarus to serve him and his family. This dismissive attitude was baked into society; the rich man expressed "normal" views about people. Paul taught that the gospel upended that normalcy.

Household Codes in the Greco-Roman World

As we move into the household codes specifically, I encourage readers today to be alert to how the gospel challenges the social world of the first century. We have seen how Paul re-imagines the important social custom of banquet or community dinner, undercutting the social hierarchy based on Christ's inclusive redemptive work on the cross. We can be too quick to assume that marriage, for example, is similarly expressed across cultures, and so we make assumptions and then miss the impact of Paul's teaching. Also, we might be tempted to isolate one of these pairs, but that minimizes the larger social structure that informed each pair, namely hierarchy of social worth. Therefore, we will spend a bit of time looking at ancient customs surrounding the household, including marriage, parenting, and the institution of slavery.

The household codes found in Ephesians (see also Colossians and 1 Peter) grew from Plato and Aristotle's teachings on what they saw as natural hierarchy within human societies. Women were understood to be inferior to men, and some groups were deemed natural slaves to serve superiors (i.e., Greeks, according to Aristotle). Women had different virtues than men, and slaves were "naturally" deficient in virtue. Aristotle believed that a wife showed womanly courage by subordinating herself to her husband, and a slave could understand reason if spoken by his or her owner (*Politics* 1260a; *Eth. nic.* 8.11.6–7).

These ideas continued with some modification into Paul's day, including more emphasis on social and philosophical questions, less on politics and family. The patriarchal perspective, that a man/husband is superior to a woman/wife, permeated the culture.[5] For example, the first-century Stoic philosopher Gaius Musonius Rufus urged husbands to uphold self-control as the stronger one of the pair and superior in character.[6] For example, M. Rufus urges wives to study philosophy, which sounds progressive. Yet his rationale for such study is so that a husband has a more pleasant wife and home. The modern philosopher Martha Nussbaum points out that M. Rufus failed to consider the sphere of life in which a virtue was demonstrated. The male sphere of statecraft and military was superior to the female sphere of the domestic.[7] Moreover, by neglecting actual social conditions, Stoics exposed their blind spot as they accepted embedded systems of power. A similar gaping blind spot, racism, affected both abolitionists and the pro-slavery parties in the United States.[8] The main point of the brief history lesson is that patriarchy was pervasive, women were understood as inferior to men, and a social hierarchy that seemed both natural and essential to an orderly society was in place. Within these general and broad perimeters, women had some agency, could speak publicly without accusations of immodesty in some circumstances, and could be patrons, as well as civic and religious leaders.[9]

---

5. Plutarch, *Advice to the Bride and Groom*, urges couples toward harmony, but this is created as the wife accedes to her husband's preferences, shares his gods, accepts his friends, and models her emotions after his.

6. Musonius Rufus, Lecture XII, "On Sexual Indulgence." See also Hering, *Colossian and Ephesian* Haustafeln, 246–52. For a translation, see Lutz, *Musonius Rufus*.

7. Nussbaum concludes, "here we encounter a limitation that Musonius shares with many other Stoics: the failure to understand the extent to which human dignity and self-respect require support from the social world." Nussbaum, "Incomplete Feminism," 302.

8. For an excellent historical analysis of pre-civil war biblical exegesis and hermeneutics on slavery, see Noll, *Civil War as a Theological Crisis*. Noll cites Philip Schaff, a German theologian who, perceptively pointed to the underlying issue with American slavery: "*The negro question lies far deeper than the slavery question.*" Noll, *Civil War as a Theological Crisis*, 51.

9. Hylen, *Finding Phoebe*. See also Hylen, *Women in the New Testament World*. See also Cohick, *Women in the World of the Earliest Christians*.

In the ancient society at large, and in Christian congregations, one found widows and widowers, orphans, freed men and women, and slaves, all of whom would not fall under the category of married. You might find a divorced husband who also lost a child to death, or a widow who married a widower with children, or a freed woman who had married and is now a widow, or an adult child with neither parent living. The categories of the household codes are general and abstract, and the actual social world was much more complex, as real human communities tend to be. Churches today include blended families, widows and divorced people, single parents. Paul is not setting up marriage here as an ideal (he is very positive about the single life; see 1 Cor 7:25–40). He writes about marriage, parents and children, and slavery because these are the three categories that make up the archetype family, and because the home is both the physical space in which the church met and is a metaphor for understanding the church as the family of God. He is not affirming the culture, but challenges its structures with the counter-cultural gospel of Christ our peace. In this, Paul fills out what he declared earlier, that believers are members of God's household (2:29) and are God's beloved children (5:1).

Ephesians 5:22–24

In many modern Bibles, the editors place a subheading between 5:21 and 5:22, or at least begin a new paragraph. However, there are two reasons for considering these verses to be tightly linked. First, Paul does not follow his typical practice of using a conjunction when beginning a new topic. Because 5:22 lacks a conjunction, we are on solid ground in claiming that Paul intended 5:21 to inform 5:22 and the rest of the household codes.

Second, Paul implies the participle "submitting" in 5:22, taking it from 5:21. Said another way, a literal reading of 5:22 is "wives to your own husbands as to the Lord."[10] Is Paul qualifying 5:21 by saying that husbands do not need to submit to their wives, or does Paul explain the sort of submission requested by wives, namely that it is the same as what is required of all believers out of reverence for Christ? The former conclusion reads more

10. The verb is missing in P46 and B, two very early Alexandrian manuscripts, and Jerome indicates the verb is absent in the Greek codices (Heine, *Commentaries of Origen and Jerome*, 233). The third-person imperative is found in several early manuscripts, but this raises the question as to why Paul would address children and slaves directly (second-person plural) but speak generally to the whole congregation about wives (third-person plural). For a helpful discussion, see Thielman, *Ephesians*, 392–93.

into the text, for if this was Paul's intention, we would expect him to have repeated "to submit" in an indicative or imperative form. The verb is a participle, not an imperative. Nor in 5:24 does Paul use the imperative when he asks wives to submit to their husbands; instead, the indicative verb is only used in the clause that speaks of the church submitting to Christ, and is assumed, not repeated, in the second clause, as it is in some English translations. Nor does Paul command that wives obey their husbands, although this was the common expectation at the time. Plutarch provides one of the two other places where we find the call for a wife to submit; typically, he uses the verb "obey."[11]

The Greco-Roman society took for granted that everyone would submit to someone else in some fashion, as even the emperor submitted to the gods. But could a father submit to his child, or an owner to her slave? Because the system assumed an asymmetrical relationship and social worth between the superordinate and the subordinate, with the latter submitting to maintain the honor of the former, the simple answer is "no." But we have seen already that Paul's gospel message does not embrace the culture's social evaluation of people. Paul remakes the household power dynamics in line with the equality and mutuality all share in Christ. In this, Paul fills out what he declared earlier, that believers are members of God's household (2:29) and are God's beloved children (5:1).

Order within the Christian community is maintained as each looks out for the needs of the other; there is no need for a hierarchy of social worth based on the implied or stated standard of a free male. Would Paul then be assuming in 5:21 that a husband submitted to his wife? I think the answer is both "no" and "yes." Paul would not assume a husband could submit to his wife from a legal standpoint, for example, since she was a "minor" who needed a male guardian to represent her in court. But Paul would expect a husband to functionally submit to his wife in that he commands a type of love, a self-sacrificial love, that requires husbands to give up the social honor society says they deserve.

Paul qualifies the submission *as to the Lord*. This phrase does not imply that the wife submits to her husband as though he was Christ or lord

---

11. Plutarch, *Conj.* 11 uses terms such as ἡγεμονία and προαίρεσις and κρατεῖν (passage 33). The verb "to submit" is used in *Conj.* 33. See also Ps. Callisthenes (ca. 100 BCE), *A Narrative, Remarkable and Really Marvelous, of the Lord of the World, Alexander the King* (*Hist. Alex. Magni* i. 22.4) I.22.19–20. The text explains that Alexander the Great speaks to his mother after his father, Philip, wronged her, "It is proper for the wife to be submissive to her own husband" (translation in Balch, *Let Wives Be Submissive*, 98).

to her. Nor is Paul indicating that the wife shows her submission to Christ by submitting to her husband, for he is not an intermediary between his wife and her Lord. Rather, Paul circumscribes the wife's submission to that which would be asked by the loving, always faithful, self-sacrificial Lord Jesus Christ, who came not to be served but to serve (Mark 10:45). Paul stresses the distinction between husband and Christ with the conjunction beginning 5:24. The Greek term is *alla*, an adversive conjunction meaning "but" or "on the contrary," which makes clear that "savior" is exclusive to Christ; husbands are not in any way responsible for the salvation or sanctification of their wives.

In 5:23, Paul employs a metaphor using head and body. A metaphor is a figure of speech that brings two different subjects together to form a new thought. A metaphor is not a propositional statement nor a flowery way to offer a literal statement. For example, Paul is not speaking of "headship" here, for "headship" is a propositional statement, while Paul creates a metaphor. In Paul's day, the metaphor of head and body joined two things that were similar (both part of a human) and dissimilar (the head had more honor). The social honor linked with ontological values of mind over material, head over body. The social and ontological were then viewed through a gendered lens, with male as mind and female as body. As Aristotle declared, female was inferior to male in an ontological, social, and rhetorical sense.

Is this the picture Paul reinforces? Because the definition of "head" is contentious, we turn first to the second half of 5:23 for guidance. Christ is described as head, which is then qualified as savior.[12] Paul describes Christ as the head of his body, a function that causes the body to grow and develop (1:22–23; 4:15–16; see also Col 2:19). As such, husbands are brides, for they are members of the church, of which Jesus Christ is the (only) savior. Jesus's saving act was self-sacrificial, a giving up of himself in love (5:2), on the cross, making peace (1:7; 2:15). In juxtaposing "head" and "savior," Paul defines the former as self-giving love, for the latter, savior, speaks of redemption and deliverance, not "leadership."

Left to discuss is the description of the husband as "head." In Greek, *kephalē* overwhelming refers to the physical head that sits on one's neck. In a metaphoric sense, *kephalē* can mean preeminence, or source, or can serve as a synecdoche for the whole; however, its definition as leader is

---

12. Christ is rarely called savior (John 4:42; Phil 3:20–21), perhaps because Roman emperors and generals were frequently addressed as savior. Some emperors also held the title "son of god," while Paul clearly distinguishes Jesus Christ as the one who sits at God's right hand (2:6), who is the true Son of God (4:13).

highly contested.[13] Wayne Grudem, who advocates for "leader" as the meaning of *kephalē* here, finds that 87 percent of ancient references refer to the physical head, 3 percent refer to a starting point or top, and 5 percent are metaphorical, with 2 percent using *kephalē* as leader.[14] However, this 2 percent includes the Greek translation of the Hebrew Bible, and Hebrew did use "head" metaphorically to mean "leader."[15] Removing the Septuagint references, because it is a translation and not an indigenous Greek text, drops the percentage even lower. In the end, if less than 2 percent of the occurrences of *kephalē* refer to a leader, why would Paul assume that his Ephesian readers, most of whom are gentile Greek speakers, not Jewish Hebrew speakers, would understand "leader" when they heard *kephalē*?[16]

Church fathers speak of *kephalē* as meaning source. Using three examples from the fourth century, we turn first to Athanasius, bishop of Alexandria, who writes on 1 Cor 11:3, "the Son is the Head, namely the beginning of all· and God is the Head, namely the beginning of Christ; for thus to one unbegun beginning of the universe do we religiously refer all things through the Son."[17] Archbishop Cyril of Alexandria highlights Adam as the first head of the human race, and Christ as the second Adam, the head, the source of all who are immortal in him. Cyril continues,

> Yet he though God by nature, has himself a generating head, the heavenly Father and he himself, though God according to his nature, yet being the Word, was begotten of him. Because head means source, he establishes the truth for those who are wavering in their mind that man is the head of woman, for she was taken out of him. Therefore, as God according to his nature, the one Christ and Son and Lord has as his head the heavenly Father, having

---

13. On κεφαλή, see BDAG 542. Liddell and Scott Lexicon (1843, 9th ed., 1996) has over twenty-five entries under κεφαλή, including the metaphorical meaning "source," but no entry referring to "leader" or "authority over." Ancient lexicons do not define κεφαλή as authority or leader; see Cervin, "Does *kephalē* Mean 'Source' or 'Authority Over'?," 85–112. See also Fee, *First Epistle to the Corinthians*, 502–3; Thiselton, *First Epistle to the Corinthians*, 812–22; Westfall, "This Is a Great Metaphor!," 587.

14. Grudem, "Does *kephalē* ('Head') Mean "Source' or 'Authority Over'?," 38–59.

15. The Septuagint typically translates the Hebrew (*rōš*) "head" if used metaphorically as "leader" with the term *archōn*, not *kephalē*.

16. Colossians 2:9–10 speaks of Christ as *kephalē* over all rulers and authorities, for within his body dwells the fullness of deity. Paul's point is that Christ is the source of life for believers, he is the source of all things because he is fully God.

17. Athanasius, *Syn.* 2.27, Anathema 26. *Select Works and Letters of Athanasius*, 465.

himself become our head because he is of the same stock according to the flesh.[18]

Finally, Chrysostom, bishop of Constantinople, insists in his reading of 1 Cor 11:3 that Christ the Son is of the same substance with the Father. Like Cyril, Chrysostom speaks against the heretical position that Christ is a subordinate being to the Father. He adds that if Paul wanted to say that the Father was the ruler, Paul would have chosen the owner/slave pair, not the male/female pair.[19]

Examples of *kephalē* as preeminent occur within political dialogue. The emperor might be portrayed as *kephalē* and his subjects as his body. In this case, the body is to give its life for the head.[20] The *kephalē* of the soldier is protected in battle, for while the body might live without a limb, it cannot survive without its *kephalē*. So too, the general or emperor was protected as having pride of place, with the body members willing to die to save the head. Michelle Lee-Barnewall points out Paul's great reversal of this metaphor, for it is the head, Christ, that dies, so that the body might live.[21] Jesus makes this point when he admonished the disciples against following gentile leadership models (Matt 20:25–28). Jesus says that the gentile rulers lord over their subjects, but it must not be that way among the disciples. The one who wishes to be great, must be the servant, the slave, of others. I must point out that Jesus does not use the term "servant-leader"; just *diakonos* (servant), just *doulos* (slave).

The two verses addressed to the wife submitting end with the potentially sobering phrase, "in everything." This phrase has been wrongly interpreted as removing women's agency, as taking away her right to say "no." Paul is not saying that the husband's sexual, financial, recreational, familial, or any other preferences take priority over his wife's preferences. Instead, Paul imagines that as the husband submits to Christ, and thus finds joy in doing good works with a full heart for his gentle savior, so too his wife

18. Cyril of Alexandria, *Arcad.* 5.6 (translation in Westfall, *Paul and Gender*, 86n69).

19. Chrysostom, *Homilies on First Corinthians*, Homily 26.3. Aristotle, *Pol* 1255b, compares the master with soul and the slave with body, and argues that this symbiotic relationship is beneficial for both, because "the slave is a part of the master—he is, as it were, a part of the body, alive yet separated from it." Translation in Hering, *Colossian and Ephesian* Haustafeln, 224.

20. Seneca, *De clementia* 2.2.1, speaks this way of Nero.

21. Lee-Barnewall, "Turning ΚΕΦΑΛΗ on Its Head," 605–8.

would find honoring and respecting her husband can be done with a full heart because he loves her with a full, self-sacrificial heart.

Ephesians 5:25–33

Paul turns to the husband and will command him three times to love his wife (5:25, 28, 33). The love insisted upon by Paul is different than what his wider society would have called for. This love is *agape* love, and the verb *agapaō* is never used within discussions of the household codes outside the New Testament. Paul distinguishes the Christian husband's love as self-sacrificial, as modeled on Christ. Contrast this with society's expectations that the husband would enjoy harmony in the home as the wife was loyal, obedient, modest, devoted to family and his family's gods. Pliny the Younger praises his (much younger) wife Calpurnia Hispulla for her love for him, expressed in reading and re-reading his writings. Pliny is not thinking of self-sacrifice, but self-congratulations and his wife's adulation.[22] The culture would have supported Calpurnia giving her life for him as a demonstration of her love, but men sacrificed for greater things, like victory over Rome's enemies.

It is difficult to express the magnitude of Paul's counter-cultural claim in his command that husbands love their wives as Christ loves the church. We are so used to hearing this passage that its sharp edge has been dulled with familiarity. But make no mistake, Paul is asking a *lot* of the husbands. They are asked to give up their social privilege, modeled most vividly by their crucified savior. The one who gave himself up to death on the cross modeled humility, not Roman masculinity. The latter was expressed most in exercising authority over others, including women and slaves, and in having control of a situation.[23] The way of the cross, however, embraces public shame and suffering now in expressing vulnerable love that uplifts others (Heb 12:2).

Paul continues for two verses to describe the work of Christ in salvation (5:26–27). At first glance this might seem a digression, but Paul has

22. Pliny the Younger, *Letters* 4.19, explains that his wife is "highly intelligent, and extremely frugal; she loves me, which is a sign of chastity. Her love for me has made her take up books. She reads and rereads my writings and even memorises them." Translation in Lefkowitz and Fant, *Women's Life in Greece and Rome*, 233.

23. Lee-Barnewall states, "When Paul asks husbands as heads to sacrifice themselves for their wives, he asks them to do that which goes against this fundamental order of society." Lee-Barnewall, "Turning ΚΕΦΑΛΗ on Its Head," 609.

two key points he wants to make. First, he continues to teach on the nature of the church. Recall that the household codes are linked with the house church and Paul's description of their worship (5:18–21). Paul emphasizes Christ's work in making the church holy and blameless. This is Christ's work alone, and Paul makes this clear with the reflective pronouns that link only Christ to the work of making holy. Holiness happens by washing with water through the word. Paul may have in mind baptism, for in two other places we find "the washing" tied to baptism (1 Cor 6:11; Titus 3:5). The phrase "through the word" calls to mind a liturgical setting, and we've already established that Paul connects the household codes with the house church setting. It is possible Paul alludes to a bride's bath before her wedding day, but this analogy breaks down quickly, as grooms did not give their brides baths before the wedding. A more likely allusion reflected here is from Ezekiel's vision of God's love for Israel (Ezek 16:1–43). In this passage the Lord baths Jerusalem, having claimed her as his own. He anoints her and gives her beautiful clothing. We might reflect on the new Jerusalem, the bride, the church, adorned for her husband (Rev 21:2, 9–10; see also Rev 19:7–8).

Paul's focus is on holiness and moral blamelessness. Yet some commentators extend the metaphor to comment on the physical beauty of a young bride and conflate a woman's physical beauty with her moral value. The modern church teaches, at times implicitly, that a holy woman is a slim, beautiful woman, while an ugly woman is less worthy. But is pursuit of a youthful body a godly activity? Are wrinkles and gray hair a curse to be mourned? The objectification of women is perhaps best captured by husbands (including pastors) who publicly describe their wives as "smoking hot," a reference to the Will Ferrell movie, *Talladega Nights: The Ballad of Ricky Bobby*.[24] The culture's assessment of physical beauty and sexiness has no place in determining a person's holiness, for holiness is accomplished in Christ.

Having described in detail the loving care of Christ for his church, Paul returns to focus on the husband, commanding that he ought to love his wife with the same self-sacrificial love. No mention is made of husband as head; the focus is on body, on loving his wife as his own body. Paul is building a case that will conclude with a quotation from Genesis, that the two, husband and wife, become one flesh, one body, in their marriage. By emphasizing love of one's own body, Paul pushes past seeing a wife as an

---

24. Demuth, "I'm Sick of Hearing About Your Smoking Hot Wife."

object. Instead, the husband should understand the mutual reciprocity that characterizes a marriage. Treating his wife as his own body means giving heed to her ideas, desires, ambitions, because her worth is as the husband's own worth.

Paul gives the same teaching to the Corinthians, specifically around sexual conduct. Paul states that the wife does not have authority over her body, but her husband does, *and* the husband does not have authority over his own body, but his wife does (1 Cor 7:4). I imagine several men in the congregation listening to the letter for the first time raised their hand and asked that this passage be repeated, for they could not believe their ears! The Greco-Roman culture gave a husband authority over both his own and his wife's body, and he could have sexual relations with whomever he pleased (so long as it was not another man's wife). But in Christ, the wife is her own person who has authority over her husband's body, that is, she can initiate sex or decline it. If in the most intimate area of the relationship, how much more in the quotidian acts that make up most of married life. Paul envisions a mutuality where husbands and wives love freely as they live out their marriage as one flesh.

Paul draws a further conclusion from the Genesis passage. He presents a mystery, a redemptive truth almost too amazing to comprehend: the unity of Christ and the church. This is the truth of the gospel now revealed in Christ (1:9; 3:9; 6:19). The one-flesh creation in marriage provides insight by analogy to an aspect of the church's relationship to Christ its savior, namely the closeness, the identity, that each believer and the church as a whole has because they are in Christ.

As Paul concludes his discussion on marriage, he again commands husbands to love their wives, as he loves himself. The husband cannot take advantage of society's rules that privilege his honor and social worth. Paul turns on its head (pun intended) the patriarchal hierarchy that grounded ancient marriage practices and calls for self-sacrificial love. In most English translations, the final clause in 5:33 addresses the wife. For several reasons, I'd like to suggest that a better rendering would be "so that the wife might respect her husband." First, when the New Testament household codes address specific groups, the pattern is to address one group and then move to another without returning to address the previous group.[25] Presuming that

25. Walsh and Miller write that "none of the twenty subsections of the NT household codes give instructions to a previously addressed person or to a person to be later addressed. . . . Thus, it would be unique for Eph 5.33 to go back and include another directive to wives." Walsh and Miller, "Translating Ephesians 5.33," 106.

Paul follows this pattern, he would not return to address wives in 5:33, but would conclude his admonition to husbands. Second, Paul does not use an imperative but the subjunctive when speaking of the wife. Third, Paul includes the conjunction (*hina*) that typically is translated as "in order that" or "so that."[26] Some English texts ignore the common meaning and translate the subjunctive verb tense as though it were imperative. Yet in all other cases of *hina*+subjunctive in Ephesians, the ESV translates the phrase as "so that" and uses a helping verb like "may" or "should."[27] To maintain literary patterns, to translate syntax consistently, and to give full weight to the subjunctive, 5:33 should be interpreted as addressed only to husbands—they are commanded to love their wives, so that their wives may respect them.

Ephesians 5:18–33: Reflections on Preaching and Teaching

What do we do with this teaching, that is so different from what many of us were taught? Maybe we start with what Paul said, rather than with our own presuppositions or questions. For example, in discussing husbands, Paul does not mention roles such as protector or provider. Paul does not speak of leadership or authority as part of the oneness of the marriage. What new images, pictures, metaphors, and stories, based on what Paul wants husbands to think about, can be substituted for our cultural expectations?

In discussing wives, what biblical pictures of them should we draw upon? Paul was close friends with two married couples, Priscilla and Aquila, and Junia and Andronicus (Rom 16:3, 7). In the first case, Priscilla and her husband co-led churches, and Priscilla taught Apollos, alongside her husband (Acts 18:26). In the second case, Junia and her husband preached the gospel with such vigor that they experienced the same fate as Paul, imprisonment. We could describe these marriages as mutual partnerships in service for the gospel. The wife and husband exercised gifts of preaching and teaching, and both accepted the consequences, the sufferings, resulting from such faithfulness.

We might also go back to the beginning, as Paul does, and re-examine our assumptions about the Genesis narrative. Genesis chapters 1 and 2 tell the same story of God creating the world but from two different angles,

26. The Greek reads ἡ δὲ γυνὴ ἵνα φοβῆται τὸν ἄνδρα and the δὲ need not be translated because it follows an imperative and is part of a subjunctive clause including ἵνα (BDAG 213.3).

27. Walsh and Miller, "Translating Ephesians 5.33," 105.

much like the Gospels tell the story of Jesus from four perspectives. In Genesis chapter 2, the story confirms what Genesis 1 states, namely that male and female are both made by God and made in God's image. In Gen 2:18, the woman is said to be a helper (*'ezer*) of the man. This Hebrew word means someone who completes the goal, in this case one who will help the man accomplish the task of tending the garden and filling the earth with their progeny. The term does not imply second rate or assistant level, for it is used often of God himself (Deut 33:29; Ps 121:1; Hos 13:9).[28] No mention is made of Adam's superiority because he was made first, and primogeniture does not apply here because Eve was not born, but she was made by God. Nor is there mention of Adam leading or having authority over Eve. Instead, as Paul points to in our passage, Adam is united to his wife, and the two become one flesh (2:24).

Genesis chapter 3 tells the awful story of the fall and includes the repercussion for the woman that literally reads, "your desire shall be for your husband, and he shall rule over you." Several points should be considered in explaining this sentence. First, the renowned philologist A. A. Macintosh re-examined the rare biblical term "desire" (*teshuqa*) and concluded that the word means single-minded devotion or focus (the noun appears in Gen 3:16; 4:7; Song 7:10).[29] The man's desire for his beloved is good and intimately personal (Song 7:10). So too the woman's desire is for the return to pre-fall harmony between herself and her husband. The term "desire" in Gen 4:7 depicts Sin as single-mindedly focused on causing Cain to do harm. In all three cases, the desire felt is characteristic of the being who feels it. Both men and women feel love towards another and with single-minded devotion pursue another. Sin feels desire only for power and destruction and seeks to destroy humans. Cain failed to resist but allowed Sin to rule.

Second, the woman's desire is not "against" her husband, but towards or for him. At issue is the preposition *'el*, which is typically translated as "to" or "towards." In the similar situation of Cain and Abel in Gen 4, Cain's action is towards his brother, even though it is hostile. The preposition does not make the action negative; the woman's desire is not against her husband.

Third, the husband's rule over his wife is the sad result of the fall. The husband has no need to ward off his wife's desire, for unlike Sin's attack on

28. Gupta, *Tell Her Story*, 23–26.

29. Macintosh writes, "I conclude that 'desire is not a proper rendering of the Hebrew word. . . . Rather, . . . 'concern, preoccupation, (single-minded) devotion, focus' appears to be more likely." Macintosh, "Meaning of Hebrew הקושת," 385.

Cain, the woman desires good, even as the lover in Song of Songs desires good. Said another way, Cain is asked to rule Sin, ultimately so as to destroy its effect on him; but surely the husband is not asked to rule his wife so that she is removed, destroyed, obliterated.[30]

30. Lynch, "Contrary Women."

EPHESIANS 6

Ephesians 6:1–4: Children and Parents

OF THE THREE PAIRS within the household codes, the one instructing children and parents is the shortest. Paul's message that children obey their parents is a common expectation, then and now.

Historical Setting of Children in the Greco-Roman World

But there are important qualifications about his historical context we must consider as we explore Paul's teaching here. First, Paul included as "children" anyone who had a living parent, although the primary sense of the term would be pre-adults. About 50 percent of people in their early twenties had a living father, and those individuals were under his authority. Both Jewish and pagan gentile writers emphasized the supreme importance of caring for elderly parents (see also 1 Tim 5:8), based on the greater conviction that the highest form of piety, except for the worship of the gods, was honoring, caring for, and obeying parents. Hanne Sigismund-Nielsen sums up the gentile position, "It is no exaggeration to say that pagan Roman society was built on the notion of *pietas*."[1] The first-century Jewish author Philo of Alexandria explained that parents are somewhere in between divine and human in that, like God, they gave life to their children, but as humans, they will eventually die. Therefore, children were duty-bound to respect their parents as second only to God (*Spec. laws* I.38). Many cultures today share the first century's view that children of any age should defer to their parents' wisdom. I saw this firsthand in a Bible study held by Kenyan women during my time in that country. The study looked at the tragedy of

---

1. Sigismund-Nielsen, "Vibia Perpetua," 112.

the Levite and his concubine in Judges. One conclusion drawn was that the terrible events could have been avoided had the son-in-law listened to his father and remained another night in his house (Judg 19:1–10).

Second, Paul addresses the children in the church before their parents, honoring them and their place in the Christian community. This observation may seem a small detail, but in the honor/shame culture that characterized Paul's world, protocol was everything. There is a gospel ring to Paul's ordering, putting first the one whom society says should be second. As Margaret MacDonald observes, "In Col 3:20 and Eph 6:1, the 'performative' quality of children being called out by name in the midst of the assembly *constructs* a world of belonging: children are drawn into the community and a sense of membership and allegiance is reinforced."[2]

Third, Paul addresses both free and slave children, each of whom is a co-heir with Christ and shares in an inheritance. I will say more below, but a brief note should be made here that slave children did not have a father in the typical sense of the term; they had an owner. They might not know their biological parents, but within the church, they would have surrogate parents. The free children learn that their slave sisters and brothers are of equal social worth and have the same opportunities to grow into mature, faithful believers (2:14–19; 3:6). The society called a slave boy a *filius neminis*, a son of no one, but in Christ, the slave child had an inheritance and a Father. Paul signals that every child is valued, regardless of their social class or legal status. Blake Leyerle recognizes the impact this has for children, "The first significant difference that Christianity made to the lives of children was an enhanced attention to their lives and pursuits. This surge of interest was prompted in part by their visible presence and active participation in religious rites and rituals."[3]

Fourth, the ancient world viewed a child as a miniature adult, one who with strict, careful instruction would grow upright and trustworthy as an adult.[4] The culture did not share the Western developmental view of a child who passes through stages of mental, physical, and emotional growth. With this developmental model, we assume that factors in childhood shape what the child will become, while the ancient world believed the child's

2. MacDonald, *Power of Children*, 153.

3. Leyerle, "Children and 'the Child' in Early Christianity," 566. He estimates that about 40 percent of the congregation was children.

4. Laes, *Children in the Roman Empire*, 26, suggests that about 50 percent of children did not live beyond ten years. See also Cohick, "Women, Children, and Families in the Greco-Roman World."

character was formed at birth. Child rearing was designed to develop rational thought through disciplinary methods that would be judged harsh by Western standards but reflected the overall physically violent nature of the Greco-Roman society. Most children were working in shops or fields by age seven, when their adult teeth came in. From the city of Herculaneum, which was destroyed by the eruption of Vesuvius in 68 CE, we find child skeletons as young as seven years old that show wear and tear on major upper body joints that align with repetitive motion tasks such as hoeing and rowing.[5]

Ephesians 6:1–3

Paul devotes three verses to children, including a biblical quotation. He opens with a straightforward command that children obey their parents. I should pause here to note that in the Ephesians' household codes, children and slaves are commanded to obey their parents and owners, while wives are invited to submit to their husbands. Unfortunately, some commentaries make generalizing statements that the subordinate member—wife, child, slave—obeys the superordinate, failing to give full weight to the verb "submit" and its indicative mood, not imperative, when addressing wives.[6] Paul modifies his command to children to obey with the phrase "in the Lord." The point Paul makes is not that children only need obey Christian parents, but that they obey directives that are godly. If a parent asks the child to steal, for example, the child is not obligated to do so. Even pagan philosophers would agree, as we read Musonius Rufus, a first-century thinker who declared that studying philosophy was tantamount to obeying the gods (all college philosophy professors rejoice to read this!). Should a father forbid his son to study philosophy, the son has permission to disobey his father, because the son's first duty is to Zeus, the father of all.[7]

Paul cites from the Fifth Commandment, drawing on both Exod 20:12 and Deut 5:16. Paul includes the promise that a child who obeys

5. Laes, *Children in the Roman Empire*, 153–54.

6. Lincoln, *Ephesians*, 402; Thielman writes, "Christ is the submissive party's authority, and when wives, children, and slaves render obedience, they do so out of obedience to Christ, not because of any innate authority in the male head of the household." Thielman, *Ephesians*, 376.

7. Musonius Rufus, xvi, 30–31, 104–6. See his collected and translated work in Lutz, *Musonius Rufus*.

and respects his or her parents will live. Paul speaks of this commandment as the first to offer a promise, which has raised questions as the Second Commandment also seems to hold a promise. Likely Paul intends that the promise is specific to obeying a direct command. The promise is for a long and prosperous life, which begs the question of what Paul imagines as long and prosperous. He certainly would not exclude suffering as part of this life, nor would he exclude service to others (2:10; 4:2, 12; 6:10–13). The vision cast in this promise, lived out in Christ within God's family, is one of deep joy knowing that the heavenly Father calls you his beloved (5:1). This aligns with Jesus's statements that his yoke is easy (Matt 11:30) and his way includes taking up your cross and following him (Matt 16:24).

Ephesians 6:4

Paul offers a single sentence to the fathers that both cautions and encourages (6:4). Let's start with the encouragement. Paul commands fathers to bring up their children, to nourish them with food that helps them grow (*ektrephō*). Using the same verb, Paul remarks that husbands care for their own bodies and should do likewise for their wives (5:29). We should not assume that all husbands and fathers were not caring for their wives and children; rather, we see Paul making public with his letter the importance of this value. Society gave much leeway to the father as to how he treated his children, while Paul's command to nurture them placed a gospel definition on how a responsible father should act. Jesus uses a related verb (*trephō*) when describing God's good care of the birds who neither sow nor reap but still are fed (Matt 6:26; Luke 12:24). Luke uses the verb to describe how Jesus himself was raised (Luke 4:16).

Not only are the physical needs of the children important, but also their education. Three points about education in the ancient world will help us understand Paul's message, including the importance it held in the wider society, the severity of punishment often connected with it, and the role of mothers in the education of their children. First, education was highly valued at this time, for both girls and boys, albeit they were educated in different ways and environments, with much of women's education happening in the home. Nonius Marcellus, borrowing from Marcus Terentius Varro, a first-century BCE scholar, summarized a child's education, "The midwife brings out [the child], the nurse feeds it (Latin: *educat nutrix*), the pedagogue instructs, and the schoolmaster teaches."[8] Christian Laes remarks on the link between the notions of feeding/nurturing and educating both in Latin and in the Greek. Such education continued into adulthood, as mentors and teachers continue to educate.[9]

Second, physical punishment, including whipping, was part of education, even as a father's authority could be shown by a beating with a whip.[10] This reality was based partly on the idea that children were irrational and needed strict, even violent, discipline to shape them into rational adults. There were, however, voices of moderation. Seneca, for instance, denounces the punitive nature of education and promotes a model that created courage and fortitude, as students faced hardships (for a similar rationale, see Heb 12:5–11). The Essenes, a Jewish sect, believed teaching children involved humility and kindness, and they taught Scripture and their group's traditions and practices to both girls and boys.[11]

Mothers played a key role in the education of their children. An example from the second century illuminates the context. Eudaimonis writes to her daughter-in-law, Aline, about family life. Her daughter is pregnant and Eudaimonis hopes for a boy. She remarks that Aline's daughter, who is staying with her grandmother, is doing well in her studies.[12] A similar picture can be drawn about Timothy's education from his mother, Eunice, and grandmother, Lois (2 Tim 1:5, with 3:15).

Paul focuses on fathers, not on parents, in 6:4, for they had the weight of society behind their authority.[13] Interestingly, Paul does not link the father's role with God the Father nor does he draw a parallel between a father's care and God's care for his family.[14] Part of Paul's rationale could be

8. Nonius Marcellus, *De comp. doctr.*, Lindsay; translation in Laes, "Education in Antiquity," 6.

9. Laes, "Education in Antiquity," 8.

10. Laes, *Children in the Roman Empire*, 141–43.

11. Damascus Document XIII 7–19; see Wassen, *Women in the Damascus Document*, 164–65.

12. *C.Pap.Jud.* II 442 (BL V 19; VI 24; VIII 68). Translation in Rowlandson, *Women and Society in Greek and Roman Egypt*, 121–22.

13. Saller concludes, "As the figure who exercised *potestas* over his children the paterfamilias was emphatically male. But in its barest sense, *pater familias* was used by jurists to denote no more than a property owner *sui iuris*, (of his own right) and by extension subsumed female owners." Saller, "*Pater Familias, Mater Familias*, and the Gendered Semantics of the Roman Household," 188. Roman daughters inherited alongside sons if she had her own rights, that is, was legally independent.

14. Gundry-Volf, "The Least and the Greatest," 56.

his strong emphasis elsewhere on the unique position of God the Father to all his children in God's family. God is the Father of all families (3:14–15), and believers are members of his household (2:19). Another reason that Paul does not link and earthly father's role with the heavenly Father is that the commandment calls for children to honor both father and mother. As the child grows, in-laws and uncles and aunts, plus Christian surrogate parents, speak into his or her life, watching out for their proper development and imparting wisdom in the Lord. Remember that Paul writes to his congregation that meets in a home, the natural environment for children's education. As the children sat with parents and other adults, they sang, made music, offered thanksgiving, and were invited to submit to their playmates as to Christ. Margaret MacDonald concludes that the church's efforts in educating children was "a determining factor in the shape and growth of early Christianity."[15]

Ephesians 6:1–4: Reflections on Preaching and Teaching

Honor and responsibility are the key themes in this passage. Respect is due to those who serve as fathers and mothers to those who are younger. Responsibility must be taken by those who function as fathers and mothers to those under their care. The impact of this teaching goes beyond biological or nuclear family, for the whole church must support the education and upbringing of the children in their midst. In Paul's community, "children" would include anyone who was younger than the person who served as their elder. A thirty-year-old son obeyed his mother and father; therefore, this passage encourages generational engagement within the church.

It is a tragic reality that children are vulnerable to exploitation, then and now. Unlike the sanctioned sexual exploitation of children in the Greco-Roman world, Old Testament ethics forbade the sexual use of slaves, and Jewish authors in the first century echoed this condemnation.[16] The church followed suit, which entailed critiquing an accepted gentile practice. The ramifications for Christian children's sense of self-worth are impossible to calculate. Sadly, there is still much work to be done against modern sex trafficking, domestic violence, incest, and pederasty, and the church's witness has been deeply stained through its failure to address the crimes

15. MacDonald, *Power of Children*, 151.

16. Philo, *Abr.* 133; *Spec.* 3, 37–42; *Contempl.* 60–62; Josephus, *Ant.* 1, 200–201; *Ag. Ap.* 2.37 §§273–75. See also the second-century Christian texts: Did. 2:2; Barn. 10:8.

and condemn the perpetrators. Teaching on these few verses in Ephesians requires lament and humility, and a commitment to repent and live with integrity and holiness.

Without discounting the importance of honoring parents, this moral value has been put to the test in the church's history. For example, in the early centuries, some Christian martyrs had choices to make between following their parents' commands and following Christ. For example, Perpetua's story includes several public altercations with her pagan father, who begs her to recant her faith and save the family honor. She declares, "I am a Christian," and is martyred for her testimony in 203 CE. Augustine, bishop of Hippo, eulogizes her witness, declaring that her father was used by the devil to entice her from her faith, and so it was to the devil that she showed her disloyalty, not directly to her father.[17] In the 1980s, I was part of a Cambodian church made up primarily of refugees from the Pol Pot's Khmer Rouge government and their genocidal policies. One young woman accepted Christ as her savior and matriculated at a Christian college. She received a letter from her parents stating that they disowned her. They wanted nothing to do with her and had destroyed all photos and evidence of her existence as a family member because she had chosen Christ against the wishes of her family. Throughout church history, Jesus's words that families will split because of contested loyalties have proven painfully true (Luke 12:51–53; see also Mic 7:1–7).

Ephesians 6:5–9: Slavery and Racism

As we approach the third and final pair within the household codes, we must do so with the acknowledgement that interpretations of these five verses have done immeasurable harm to individuals and the witness of the church. The story told by theologian Howard Thurman about his grandmother's experiences with preaching on certain Pauline texts reflects this point. Nancy Ambrose was born a slave and was not taught to read or write. Dr. Thurman recalls reading the Bible to her several times a week, but never from Paul's epistles. After some years, he gathered his courage to ask her why she did not want to hear from Paul's letters. Her reply captures the experience of so many African Americans who experience the racism that still pervades our society. Her owner would only allow white preachers to speak to his slaves, and these preachers would draw on Paul's text. "At least

17. Augustine, Sermon 281.2, in *The Works of Saint Augustine* III/18, 78–79.

three or four times a year he used as a text: 'Slaves, be obedient to them that are your masters, as unto Christ'. Then he would go on to show how it was God's will that we were slaves, and how, if we were good and happy slaves, God would bless us. I promised my Maker that if I ever learned to read and if freedom ever came, I would not read that part of the Bible."[18] Lisa Bowens explores the African American history of interpretation, finding examples of "the surprisingly provocative and powerful ways in which African Americans 'rescue' Paul from the clutches of white supremacy [and] speak in profound ways to the power of black faith, the ability of black resilience, and the fortitude of black intelligentsia."[19]

I think this is one of the hardest passages in Scripture for American Christians to read—or at least it should be. Our history of racialized, institutionalized slavery haunts us to this day, a slavery based on a myth of triumphant whiteness. I am cognizant of my white skin color. In a recent hermeneutics class that I taught, an African American female pastor spoke about her frustration at Paul's lack of response to slavery. I respect her opinion, and my exegesis of this passage will not be able to do full justice to the complexity of the ancient institution of slavery, nor its modern counterparts. Moreover, I can only weep at the way this passage has been used to promote violence, and a particular form of violence in our country—racism. I would have loved for Paul to SHOUT against the institution of slavery in his household codes section.

Historical Setting for Slavery in the Greco-Roman World

There is no shouting, but I do believe Paul destroys the foundations on which slavery was built, for it was built on the practice of domination by some over others. Paul's main thrust in his discussion about slavery is gospel redemption, the full salvation of forgiveness of sins (1:7) and a new humanity created in Christ (2:14–16), of believers seated with Christ (2:6), no longer in the clutches of the ruler of the power of the air (2:2). Paul has made clear that the current age is one dominated by evil forces that foster disobedience. As such, the gospel inherently pushes against the political and economic status quo and raises up those who are shamed and harmed by the entrenched powers. Esau McCaulley observed this conviction in Galatians, as Paul identifies believers living in the present evil age (Gal 1:4),

18. Bowens, *African American Readings of Paul*, 1.

19. Bowens, *African American Readings of Paul*, 2.

and this includes the evil institution of slavery, sustained by the powers of the evil age, as seen in evil laws and rulers.[20] Ephesians makes clear that Christ has overcome these forces (1:21). Paul writes his message to slaves and owners with this understanding of our spiritual world at the top of his mind, for directly after speaking to owners, Paul calls all believers to put on God's armor (6:10–13).

The Roman institution of slavery is defined by Orlando Patterson as *"the permanent, violent domination of natally alienated and generally dishonored persons."*[21] Patterson highlights several key aspects of slavery in the ancient world. First, it was permanent, inasmuch as the stain of social worthlessness stayed with the individual even if they became a freed person. Second, and relatedly, there was not two categories, slave and free, but a middle category, freedman or freedwoman. No one who had been enslaved ever made it past the "freed" rung on the ladder. A freed person owed allegiance, honor, and often a portion of their earnings to their previous owner who now functioned more as a patron. Third, the institution was based on violence: physical, emotional, mental violence. The ancient treatment of slaves turns one's stomach. Fourth, slaves had no natural families. The children they bore, the loves which they held, could be torn from them at any time. Indeed, it was common for owners both to encourage love between slaves, and then use potential separation as a threat to control behavior. Fifth, slaves had no social honor. A slave was invisible as a person. As Patterson remarks, the slave was the "ultimate human tool, as imprintable [*sic*] and as disposable as the master wished."[22]

Some interpreters suggest we look at this section on slavery from the standpoint of the roles that the slave and owner performed. In this approach, Paul affirms each role as important for the functioning of the society, and the emphasis is often on order and lines of authority. Slaves have equal worth before God, the theory holds, but different social responsibilities. This approach faces two problems. First, it covers up the social reality that slaves were the legal property of another human. They had no rights and were regularly beaten and sexually assaulted—the casual way

---

20. McCaulley writes that Christ's work includes defeating God's enemies, the spiritual forces that influence human society. "For this reason, our modern delineation between spiritual and political evil when read back into Paul's though is an anachronism." McCaulley, *Reading While Black*, 59.

21. Patterson, *Slavery and Social Death*, 13.

22. Patterson, *Slavery and Social Death*, 27.

such treatment was meted out and written about demonstrates its ubiquity.[23] The owner (male or female) dominated the slave, for the institution of slavery is one of domination. Second, it overlooks the fact that the actual duties or roles of slaves were often no different than what free men and women did. The distinction between slave and owner was not at the level of responsibilities, as though we are talking about a company executive and a dock worker. It is a matter of one individual dominating another, with the full weight of the legal and cultural systems behind them.

Perhaps an analogy would illustrate my point. If we were to transpose our traffic system onto the hierarchical household codes, we might say that when approaching a stop sign, the German-made cars may sail right through, the Japanese cars must roll slowing through, and the American-made cars must count for thirty seconds before proceeding. In this analogy, while traffic rules create order, they are also hierarchical and prejudicial. They apply differently depending on the make and model of the car. The hierarchy based on car brand in this illustration is of man-made objects, while the household codes create hierarchies of human self-worth.

The hierarchy embedded in the household codes was patriarchal and ethnocentric. Aristotle, who is responsible for its basic structure, believed that some groups of people were born slaves. Their culture lacked the sophistication of his Athenian city-state, and thus as barbarians, they were suited to serve those who knew best how to run society. In Paul's day, the household codes operationalized society's convictions that slaves were ontologically less human, and women were less rational than men. Paul took those social forms and re-defined them in light of the gospel. Paul does something similar in Galatians when he declares that in Christ there is neither Jew nor Greek, slave nor free, male and female (Gal 3:28; see also 1 Cor 12:13; Col 3:11). Paul does not remove differences between the pairs, but as Brad Braxton observes, Paul asserts "the obliteration of *dominance*."[24] Today, when interpreters focus on authority levels as the distinguishing factor between the subordinate and superordinate members of each pair, they fail to credit sexist and racial prejudices.

---

23. Shelton and Ripat, *As the Romans Did*, 217–48.

24. Braxton, *No Longer Slaves*, 94. He writes, "Many African Americans would share Paul's understanding of unity, namely that unity is not an antithesis (either/or) but rather a dialectic (both/and)" (69).

Ephesians 6:5–8

As we look closely at the biblical text, I suggest that the New Testament, including Ephesians, makes a case against the institution of slavery. Unfortunately for us, not with a direct pronouncement: END SLAVERY, but with a theological argument that undercuts the institution by giving slaves a family, an inheritance, and their personhood in Christ. Our first two pairs of the household codes were joined by at least affection, if not love. The third pair is joined through violence, with the master having complete power over the slave. One can point to exceptions, where masters were kind and slaves ate better than some free born in the community. But these individual cases do not alter the institution itself, which is built on and sustained using violence by one human to another human.

Turning to 6:5–8, I cannot overemphasize the importance of Paul speaking directly to slaves. In so doing, Paul acknowledges them; we might say "he sees them." I am unaware of any author outside the Bible who does so. Moreover, Paul addresses them *first* and then their masters, another honor bestowed. It is possible that Paul's own Roman citizenship is based on a previous enslavement. His father or grandfather could have been enslaved during Pompey's crackdown in 63 BCE or when the Roman governor Varus put down a revolt in 4 BCE. An owner could put in his or her will that their slave should be manumitted on the owner's death and given Roman citizenship if the owner was a citizen.

Within these five verses, Paul emphasizes Christ as Lord and uses the various meanings of *kyrios* (lord) as a play on words to drive home the distinction between earthly lords and the crucified and risen Lord. In 6:5, Paul qualifies in a negative way a human owner (lord) with the phrase, "according to the flesh," which removes the special honor that owners enjoyed within the wider culture. The term "flesh" in Ephesians can be neutral (5:29), but is often negative (2:3, 11). Paul continues that slaves obey, the same verb used to speak of children obeying parents. The slave is to obey with fear and trembling. This phrase can be understood in two ways. First, Paul uses this phrase when speaking about all believers' posture towards God when he asks the Philippians to work out their salvation with fear and trembling (Phil 2:12; see also 1 Cor 2:3; 2 Cor 7:15). The term "fear" is translated as respect or reverence in 5:21, the posture that each believer should render to the other and is used in 5:33 to describe how the wife will respect or revere a loving husband. In the broader use of the term, it typically refers to the subordinate honoring the superordinate. Second, and much more troubling, slaves fearing and trembling with the threat of violence would be all too common. Paul will not tolerate this sort of fear, and he explicitly forbids owners to threaten their slaves (6:9). That any should live in fear in their own homes is an abomination. Domestic violence, including intimidation of violence and outbursts of anger, has no place in Christian homes (or any home for that matter).

Paul continues that slaves act with a sincere heart. Does Paul agree with the wider society that slaves are lazy and deceitful? He certainly did not think that of Onesimus (Phlm 11, 13), and he addresses slaves as full members of God's family. Likely Paul is setting up the character qualities exhibited by slaves that are qualities every believer should emulate. He contrasts this with those who work only when their master is watching so as to curry favor (see also Col 3:22). He makes that clear in his final words to slaves that the Lord rewards everyone based on their actions, whether slave or free (6:8). Paul closes 6:5 with the phrase "as to Christ." Some translations add the verb "obey" or convey that thought. However, the qualification likely means what it did for wives and children, that their actions are ultimately valued by Christ. The slave owner is not a delegate for Christ, not some sort of stand-in for the Lord.

Ephesians 6:9

Paul commands the masters to do the same things to them, their slaves (6:9). The phrase "the same things" could refer to Paul's call for wholehearted service (6:7) or to the good deeds that will be rewarded (6:8). Because Paul also repeats the (admittedly common) verb "to make or do" from 6:8, he is at the very least connecting the value of the slave's work to the owner's own conduct before the Lord. The fourth-century church father Chrysostom argues that Paul commands owners to serve their slaves.[25] He declares that the master too must act with fear and trembling before God, his Master, that he might not be judged by God to have neglected his slaves. Chrysostom points to Jesus's words that with the measure you use, so will you be measured (Matt 7:2). He warns that the parable of the wicked servant who was forgiven his debt but would not forgive others might be applied to a harsh owner (Matt 18:32). The owner will be judged by the law of God, which is no respecter of persons and shows no favoritism.

---

25. Chrysostom, Homily 22 on Ephesians; *Eph.* 6:9; PG 62:157.

Paul continues with the participle "do not" or "stop" and adds the noun "threat" with the sense of threatening punishment. Paul insists that owners not threaten their slaves because they are both slaves before their Master in heaven. With this restriction, Paul strikes a fatal blow to the institution of slavery. The power to dominate has been removed, and with it the institution has no enforcement power. This should have radical social implications, but it would be centuries before the church listened to its call. Indeed, even today, there are those who would qualify Paul's message, stating that Paul would have allowed for some threatening, if the slave would not follow orders.[26] Paul says no such thing; his prohibition is absolute. This is important to emphasize because Paul draws a connection with God's character. Paul's line of thinking goes like this: owners cannot threaten slaves, because such threats presuppose a superior worth of the master over the slave. Such an assessment is wrong, and owners' actions must be in line with God's view that no human has permission to threaten another. God is not like a Roman master, who lords it over others; God is the Master (*kyrios*) who calls believers his children (5:1). Christ is the Lord (*kyrios*), crucified, resurrected, ascended, and will return for his people (1:7; 2:5–6; Phil 3:20–21).

Ephesians 6:5–9: Reflections on Preaching and Teaching

Paul warns the slave master that his Master does not play favorites. This refrain—God shows no favoritism—resounds throughout the New Testament. But Christ does side with the vulnerable, the widow and orphan, those in need (Matt 25:34–46). God's great redemption story includes leading his people from slavery in Egypt, and this freedom note rings throughout the Old Testament. For example, the fourth commandment to keep the Sabbath has a lengthy rationale that lists all who should not work, including one's children, slaves/servants, and foreign residents, plus farm animals. God declares that with a mighty hand he brought his people out of slavery in Egypt, thus they must keep the Sabbath to the Lord (Deut 5:13–15). God is a God who frees, so that his people might worship him fully and without restrictions. Believers are freed from sin (Eph 1:7) and freed into a new humanity in Christ (2:14–16). Paul proclaimed a gospel message that landed

26. Hoehner, *Ephesians*, 814, assumes Paul makes an implicit exception to the owner whose slave did wrong. He concludes that if the owner did not have some power to threaten, the slave might refuse to work.

him in chains, as he threatened the social and political ideology of his day. The Thessalonians saw the danger to their myth of earthly power based in Rome, for Paul proclaimed a kingdom with no hierarchies, whose king is a crucified, risen, and ascended Lord (Acts 17:5–9). What could be more provocative to the social system than an owner serving her slave, than the community choosing a slave as their leader.[27] In this, the believer would be following the example of her or his Lord, who though being in very nature God yet took up the very nature of a slave (Phil 2:6–8), coming to serve, not to be served, and give his life as a ransom for many (Mark 10:45).

Today, our American society is shaped to favor white persons over people of color, to favor Protestants over Catholics and Jews, the wealthy over the middle class and poor. We need to embrace the profound truth that God shows no favoritism. Reconciliation in Christ between all believers reminds us that not only is the individual redeemed by the cross, but the cross creates a new humanity. We must all live into that new reality.

Paul expands on the identity of the believers who are slaves within the Roman institution of slavery. He re-defines them as being slaves of Christ, a description he uses of himself in several letters (Rom 1:1; 2 Cor 4:5; Gal 1:10; Phil 1:1; Titus 1:1), as does James (Jas 1:1), Peter (2 Pet 1:1), and Jude (Jude 1:1). And Paul declares that every believer is a slave to righteousness, having been formerly a slave of sin (Rom 6:19). Paul draws on the Old Testament metaphorical use of slave or servant of the Lord ('ebed YHWH), with Moses perhaps being the best known (Num 12:7; see also Jer 25:4; Ezek 38:17). The Israelites postured themselves as God's servants who would obey his commandments, for God brought them out of slavery into the land flowing with milk and honey. Without ignoring the brutal reality of the human institution of slavery, Paul's reclassification of slaves as slaves of the Lord brings a dignity to these believers that the wider social world would deny. Paul re-frames slaves' actions so that their deeds, and how they do their deeds, becomes a model of discipleship that anyone, including their master, can emulate. Paul indicates that slaves can do the will of God (6:6), can serve wholeheartedly (6:7), and thus can be role models in the church. Paul concludes his comments to slaves with the sure promise that God rewards good deeds (6:8; see also 2 Cor 5:10). Paul indicated earlier in the letter that each believer is God's handiwork and good works have been prepared for each to walk in. That includes the slave, the one whom society

27. Church tradition holds that Onesimus was bishop of Ephesus. See Ignatius, *Ephesians* 1.3 and *Apostolic Constitutions* 7.46.

has devalued as a "thing" that has little to no moral character and whose body is a tool for hard work and sexual exploitation. This is the gospel at work transforming hierarchical configurations of social worth to celebrate all believers in Christ.

How might the early church have lived this truth? I can offer at least two examples. First, we know that slaves were given leadership roles. I have already mentioned Onesimus as the bishop in Ephesus.[28] A second example comes from the early second century in a letter by Pliny the Younger to the Emperor Trajan (*Letter* 10.96). In it, he asks about people who said they were Christians but have since recanted, whether they should still be punished as he punishes those who confess Christ. He mentions that he tortured two female slaves who have the title "deaconess" to try to get details of this "superstition." It was common to beat slaves before they testified, because they were believed to lie unless beaten. The church viewed these slave women as their leaders, and like the apostles who accepted beatings for the sake of Christ, these women leaders gave the same testimony (Acts 5:29–41).

Second, the repeated insistence on sexual morality, and the condemnation of visiting prostitutes (1 Cor 6:15), sent a strong message that the sexual promiscuity permitted for Roman men was not tolerated in the church.[29] This meant that slave owners in the church should not have sex with their slaves, even if the wider society saw nothing wrong with that practice. And this meant that no moral condemnation fell on those slaves whose masters exploited them sexually. I think it likely that Paul drew on Deut 22:25–27, which assumes that an unprotected, non-consenting woman who is seized and raped is not guilty of sexual immorality. Certainly, a female (or male) slave falls into the category of "unprotected." Sandra Richter concludes that the Deuteronomistic law "shows no interest in the victimization of an innocent party.... Nor does deuteronomic law require a woman to marry her rapist. Deuteronomic law executes the rapist."[30] I have had college students say that a slave should have resisted to the point of death. Deuteronomy says that the victim's life is precious to God, and their sexual exploitation is

28. See n27 above.

29. This section of Scripture has been used to shame women as part of the language and ideology of the purity culture. For a critique of this harmful interpretation, see Gregoire et al., *Great Sex Rescue*.

30. Richter, "Rape in Israel's World ... and Ours," 71.

not a death sentence. Paul draws the same conclusion and leaves no room for sexual predators within the body of Christ.[31]

Ephesians 6:10–24: Put on the Armor of God

As Paul finishes his letter to the Ephesians, he brings to a close his grand narrative of God's redemption plan, pulling together various threads throughout the epistle. Recall that Paul opened his letter by gesturing back before time, to God's salvation plan that involved God the Son as the one who brought forgiveness of sins and created a new people through his death, resurrection, and ascension. The plan is bigger than human redemption and includes establishing complete victory over all spiritual entities and forces, including those that plague our world now. The plan continues to unfold, with Jew and gentile brought together into one family, of which God is Father. And the powers and principalities marvel at God's wisdom revealed in this redemptive plan. Each believer, sealed with the Holy Spirit, awaits the consummation of their promised inheritance. At the end of the epistle, Paul pauses to attend to this moment, the present. This moment or age does not enjoy the full reign of Christ over all things, although the war has been won. Skirmishes and guerilla attacks by God's enemies present a constant threat. Thus, Paul closes his missive with a final word about God's protection for his people, which creates a note of hope that all shall be well.

Paul knows that as yet, not all is well, but believers have the means by which to live confidently. Paul does not shy away from detailing the evil which permeates this present age (Gal 1:4). After describing the danger, Paul offers the solution for safety, namely, putting on the armor of God. He explains the pieces of armor in terms of their spiritual value and provides a picture of the believer's actions while in armor. Paul draws extensively on Isaiah's images of the armor of God, but both he and the Ephesians would also be quite aware of Roman soldiers' gear. Even more, they would have contrasted the aggressive military force of the Romans with the call for God's righteousness and truth. They would know the difference between Christ as the true peace and the Roman *pax romana*. A defeated opponent, Calgacus, lamented that the Romans "make a desolation and call it peace" (Tacitus, *Agricola* 30.4).

---

31. For more information on sexual abuse and how to stop it, see Langberg, *Redeeming Power*. For a broader conversation, see McKnight and Barringer, *Church Called Tov*.

Ephesians 6:10–13

The opening sentences of this section are short, staccato notes that ring out much as a trumpet call signaling actions to the troops. Verses 6:10, 11, 13, and 14 include imperatives: be strong, put on (*enduō*), put on (*analambanō*), and stand. Paul uses the infinitive form of the verb "to stand" in 6:11 and both "withstand" and "to stand" in 6:13, explaining that in God's armor, believers shall be able to endure the enemy's assault. In 6:10, Paul repeats a phrase verbatim from 1:19, "in his mighty power" or "in the strength of his might." The message is for believers to actively resist the forces of evil. Think of soldiers who protect their city, which has already been won. They stand alert, attentive to the sneaky subterfuge of the enemy and ready to counter any offensive action by deceitful actors. They stand "in the Lord" likely referring to Jesus Christ. Paul is at pains throughout the epistle to emphasize the unfathomable love that empowers his victory. The irony should not be lost on us that Christ's victory was gained over Rome and all earthly and spiritual forces through the Roman instrument of torture—crucifixion. Moreover, Paul writes this from his prison cell, in chains for Christ.

The passage raises a few questions, such as what Paul intends with the phrase "day of evil" (6:13). Does it denote our present age, ruled by evil forces? Or is this day referring to a moment of crisis that believers might experience during their lives? Perhaps the phrase suggests the final judgment of Satan by Christ. We need not decide between the three options, for the armor of God would be necessary in any confrontation. Peter encourages believers to flee the devil, a figure he likens to a lion on the hunt (1 Pet 5:8–9). James speaks as Paul does, encouraging believers to stand their ground, for if they do, the devil will flee from them (Jas 4:7).

A second question follows from the first and takes its answer from it. Paul's eschatology has been adequately summarized as "now/not yet." The work of Christ is effective now and will be fully accomplished when the last enemy, death, is completely defeated and God's kingdom comes in its fullness (1 Cor 15:20–28). Because Christ is raised and we are "in Christ," therefore we share in his resurrection life. Yet because death is still active, and sin with it, believers now have need of protection as they walk worthy of their calling.

Ephesians 6:14–17

A closer look at the description of the armor of God reveals the virtues discussed throughout Ephesians. Paul speaks of truth (1:13; 4:15–25; 5:9), righteousness (4:24; 5:9), peace (2:14–18; 4:3; 6:23), the gospel (1:13; 2:17; 3:6–8), and faith (1:15; 2:8: 3:12, 17; 4:5, 13). These abstract nouns are brought to life here as pieces of armor. Believers have been encouraged to act with righteousness and faithfulness as they grow in Christ. Paul draws on Isaiah's presentation of God or his messiah bringing justice and salvation to his people and establishing peace. Isaiah 11:3–5 declares that the messiah has righteousness as his belt and faithfulness as the sash about his waist. With these virtues will he judge, so that the poor and needy will no longer suffer at the hands of the wicked. Isaiah 59:14–20 describes God's armor, his breastplate of righteousness and helmet of salvation, which represents his works of justice and salvation for his repentant people and his recompense to his enemies.

As we look at these pieces of armor individually and imagine a person putting them on, we must keep two items in mind. First, the soldier would not fight alone, but in a group. The armor protected the individual, so that the group could be more effective against the enemy. Second, while most who donned armor in Paul's day were men, as combat required physical strength, women also fought and a few commanded armies. Cleopatra VII, one of the last of the Ptolemaic rulers, was the richest person at the turn of the eras and was lover to both Julius Caesar and Marc Antony. She led her army with Antony against Octavian and committed suicide rather than face humiliation as a prisoner of Octavian, now sole ruler of the empire. Another famous woman military leader is Boudica (or Boudicea), queen of the Iceni, a group who lived in what is now Norfolk, Britain. She revolted against Roman rule and was killed in 61 CE. Artemis of the Ephesians was known for her prowess in hunting. She is often depicted with a bow and arrows. Typically, women helped protect their walled city, where they had a physical advantage of being above the enemy. The point in mentioning these examples is to say that the Ephesians would have recognized the metaphorical discussion of virtues and God's armor as pertaining to men and women.

Paul has asked believers to put on God's armor and then stand fast against the enemy, the evil forces of this dark age. He begins his description of the various pieces of armor with the belt of truth. The Roman military belt fitted around the waist and had four to eight leather straps hanging vertically from there, covering the groin or thighs. Each strap had metal studs (*bullae*), either for decoration or protection. The main purpose of the belt was to gather the loose-fitting dress that would be cumbersome to fight in. The biblical phrase "gird up your loins" is a reference to pulling one's dress in tight to the body so the legs moved freely and could maneuver well. This belt represents believers putting on truth, both the gospel truth of redemption in Christ (1:13) and the experience of this truth in their own lives (4:21, 25).

In addition to the belt of truth, believers are to put on the breastplate of righteousness (see also 1 Thess 5:8). Not only did this armor protect the wearer's vital organs, but it also signaled the individual's status. Soldiers could display their victories on the breastplate, as Caesar Augustus does in the Prima Porta Augustus statue in the Vatican Museum. Of course, most breastplates were not elaborate, as was the emperors. Instead, strips of metal were placed horizontally and held together by strips of leather, or, the more expensive option, were made of chain metal. Paul's focus is not on the model of breastplate, nor its decorations, but on the virtue of righteousness. Isaiah 59:17 LXX declares God to put on a breastplate of righteousness. In the three places in this epistle where righteousness is mentioned, so too is truth (4:24; 5:8; 6:14). Paul reminds believers that as they put on Christ, their new self is being shaped in God's truth and righteousness. Knowing truth and acting rightly or justly are sure defenses against the deceitful un-truths that harangue believers. Lies such as "you are not good enough for God's love," or "you deserve to take revenge on the one who wronged you," are undone as God's truth and justice renew believers' minds and are lived out in their relationships.

Paul continues his description of God's armor with a focus on proper footwear, so as to bring the gospel of peace. Here Paul nods to Isa 52:7 with its declaration of how beautiful on the mountains are the feet of those who bring good news and proclaim peace (see also Rom 10:15). The believers' sandals are not in focus, but what proper footwear can enable, namely the proclamation of the good news. Paul emphasizes readiness, being prepared to speak the good news to all who want to hear or to those who challenge the believer's convictions. Paul asks the Ephesians to pray that he would have such readiness so that he can fearlessly, faithfully speak the Word to the Roman authorities (6:19). And the message is that of peace. Paul earlier explains that Christ is our peace; the cross has reconciled us to God and to other believers. Christ's peace destroys hostility and builds a community of faithful family members, all children of God the Father (2:14–19).

Further protection comes from the shield of faith, which believers wield against the flaming arrows of the enemy. Roman shields were rather large, approximately two by four feet, bowed rather than flat, with the handle in the middle. The shield was made of several layers of wood, over which was placed a layer each of canvas and leather. At the edges were wrapped metal bands, and the shield might be painted or decorated. This stout, heavy item could weigh ten kilograms or twenty-two pounds. We do not have evidence that soldiers soaked their shields in water, as that would make them even heavier and would loosen the glue that holds the layers together. Instead, the metal boss at the center of the shield likely took the brunt of the stones and arrows flung at it. A word about ancient warfare helps us understand the critical role the shield played. Soldiers marched against a walled city, from which walls the defenders would throw rocks and launch burning javelins and arrows. The soldier used his shield for protection, and if it was damaged, he was exposed and defenseless. To maximize their attack against city walls, the Romans developed the *testudo* or tortoise maneuver. A unit of soldiers stood in a square of several rows. Those in the middle put their shields over their heads, while the outer ring put their shields to their sides. This encased the unit much as the turtle's shell protects it, and they could work at the base of the wall, digging out the foundations, protected from falling rocks and arrows shot from the city's defenses. Emperor Trajan's column in Rome etched this maneuver, and we read of it from the Jewish historian, Josephus, in his account of the Roman siege of Jotapata (*J.W.* 3.270). Josephus describes how the Jewish soldiers defeated the *testudo*: they poured boiling oil on the Roman soldiers, and their shields offered no protection. The Jews' victory, however, was short-lived, and Rome gained the city within a few weeks.

The Ephesians would have recognized the importance of the troops working together to defeat the enemy. The Christian's shield is not only for their personal defense, but also is to be used for the good of the group. The shield of faith probably draws attention both to Christ's own faithfulness and to believers' faith in Christ. Christ's work of redemption, the "one faith" (4:5), and Christ's faithfulness (3:12) provide complete protection against the enemy's attempts to weaken or soften God's sure promise of salvation (1:3–4). Christ's faithfulness demonstrated God's grace that saves us, and we accept that gift of grace through faith (2:8). Believers' faith should take deep root within their hearts (3:17).

The last two items in the armor of God are the helmet of salvation and the sword of the Spirit. Paul commands believers to take up these items, as though Christ is handing the helmet and sword to them. The salvation encompasses the believers' sure seat with Christ in the heavenlies (2:6), and deliverance from daily dangers faced in this present evil age. The sword of the Spirit points to the Holy Spirit's power in accomplishing the Word (*hrēma*) of God (see also 5:26). Isaiah 59:17 refers not only to the breastplate of righteousness, as we saw above, but also to the helmet of salvation, and in 59:19, the breath of the Lord. Paul likely had the larger passage in mind, as the Lord laments the lack of justice and truth, and moves to redeem Zion. The passage speaks of the Lord enacting justice, achieving salvation, and establishing truth.

While the helmet is clearly defensive protection, the sword of the Spirit should be viewed as both offensive and defensive. The word of God, the gospel of peace, challenges the kingdom of darkness and each believer can testify that in their lives the darkness was defeated. Yet it is also a defensive instrument that guards believers' minds against falsehoods by the evil one.

Ephesians 6:18–23

Paul continues his discussion about believers' preparedness in his discussion about the necessity of prayer. He no longer speaks of the armor of God, although grammatically the verses tie back to the verbs in 6:17 or 6:14. Instead, Paul addresses prayer as that necessary nourishment for all healthy armor-wearers. Believers should always pray for all the Lord's people, in all kinds of prayers, for all occasions. Four times in Greek, Paul uses the word "all." Recall Paul's description of the community's worship wherein believers, filled with the Spirit, always give thanks to the Father for everything (5:18–20). Believers are on high alert and ready to pray at any time. Jesus uses the same verb "be alert" when he warns his followers to be watchful for the day of the Lord (Mark 13:33).

Perhaps some of that urgency was based on Paul's own immediate situation. He was an ambassador in chains (6:20), waiting his audience with the Roman magistrate. He asks the Ephesians to pray for him, that he would be bold, not fearful, in speaking the mystery of the gospel (6:19). This mystery is that Jews and gentiles are united as one family of God in Christ, through his work on the cross (3:3–6). This mystery is that every believer is a member of Christ's body (5:32). Why did proclaiming such a message require boldness? Because unity in Christ spoke to each believer's equal worth in God's eyes, a direct attack on the social hierarchy that supported Roman culture. Because Christ's peace is one of self-sacrifice and love while the *pax romana* is gained and maintained by brute force.

Paul signs off with a blessing of peace to his brothers and sisters in Ephesus, as they embrace the love of Christ by faith. This love by believers towards Christ should be undying, even as they enjoy eternal life through his love. This love draws believers closer to each other and into a deeper, undying relationship to the Father and the Son.

Ephesians 6:10–23: Reflections on Preaching and Teaching

Paul makes clear in this passage that there is a battle waging, and believers are part of the fight. Said another way, Paul's point is that a believer will face direct and indirect assaults from forces empowered by evil. This terrifying reality is to be met boldly with the spiritual armament God provides. For those today who minimize spiritual forces of evil, this passage should chasten them, for they have failed to see the evil around them. For those who maximize the power of evil forces, this passage should reassure them, for God's armor provides all the protection a person, and the community, needs.

As we explore God's armor and the battle or wrestling struggle that is our Christian life, one temptation might be to give way to Christian triumphalism, or at least the rationalization of force to bring in God's kingdom. To head off such thoughts, Paul states that believers are not engaged in a battle with other humans, "flesh and blood" (6:12). Paul describes our contest as against malevolent rulers and authorities of the spiritual realm. On the one hand, we see an example of such a struggle against spiritual forces, against Satan himself, in Jesus's temptation (Matt 4:1–11; Luke 4:1–13). Satan challenged Jesus with half-truths about God's nature and Word and dangled the shiny bobble of easy, quick power in front of him. Jesus resisted the enticement to serve his own needs, creating bread to prove his Sonship. He rejected the offer of painless power in serving Satan, looking to eternal supremacy based on self-giving, obedient love. Jesus refused to make demands on God, for he knew his perfect love and did not need proof such as angels rescuing him.

On the other hand, Paul talks about his struggles with others who claim the mantel of apostle. In 2 Corinthians, he speaks candidly and passionately against those who preach a different Jesus (2 Cor 11:4). These he labels as "super-apostles" (2 Cor 11:5; 12:11); they are false apostles, disguising themselves as genuine apostles (2 Cor 11:13). In this, they simply reflect, Paul says, their real master, Satan, who disguises himself as "an angel of light" (2 Cor 11:15). Paul distinguishes his apostolic ministry as one rooted in weakness, so that God's power might be more clearly seen, including signs and miracles (2 Cor 12:9–12). Paul recognizes that although other humans sin against us, fail us, and hurt us, and behind them are institutional and systemic cultural evils. Supporting this entire malevolent structure is the one who now rules the world, Satan (Eph 2:2; Luke 4:6).

As believers learn Christ (4:20), and the Spirit recalls Scripture to their minds, they can repel wrongheaded, immature, and destructive ideas and teachings. In the heat of battle, instinct and reaction takes over. The enemy has tools at his disposal: creating self-justification and aggrandizement, rationalizing wrongs done, grumbling attitudes, fear, hopelessness, and loneliness. Paul knows that as the true, right, good, loving gospel story of God's redemption grows deep within, believers will be protected. As believers put on the armor of God, they together face an enemy with courage and confidence. Not that God's armor protects against suffering; the church martyrs' deaths put paid to such ideas. Nor is God's armor a lucky charm that keeps bad things, illnesses or disappointments in relationships or careers at bay. Instead, the armor of God, worn by the community of faith, equips them with truth, righteousness, and peace, and protects them until the end, when God brings unity to all things together in Christ (1:10).

BIBLIOGRAPHY

Athanasius. *Select Works and Letters of Athanasius, Bishop of Alexandria*. Edited by A. Robertson. NPNF 4. Grand Rapids: Eerdmans, 1980.

Augustine. *The Works of Saint Augustine: A Translation for the 21st Century, Sermons III/18 (273–305A) on the Saints*. Translation and notes by Edmund Hill. New York: New City, 1994.

Balch, David L. *Let Wives Be Submissive: The Domestic Code in 1 Peter*. Chico, CA: Scholars, 1981.

Barclay, John M. G. *Paul and the Gift*. Grand Rapids: Zondervan, 2015.

———. "Paul, the Gift, and the Battle over Gentile Circumcision: Revisiting the Logic of Galatians." *Australian Biblical Review* 58 (2010) 36–56.

Bell, Richard H. "Faith in Christ: Some Exegetical and Theological Reflections on Philippians 3:9 and Ephesians 3:12." In *The Faith of Jesus Christ*, edited by Michael F. Bird and Preston M. Sprinkle, 111–25. Peabody, MA: Hendrickson, 2009.

Best, Ernest. "Ephesians i.1." In *Text and Interpretation: Studies in the New Testament Presented to Matthew Black*, edited by Ernest Best and Robert McLean Wilson, 29–41. Cambridge: Cambridge University Press, 1979.

Billings, J. Todd. *Union with Christ: Reframing Theology and Ministry for the Church*. Grand Rapids: Baker Academic, 2011.

Bird, Michael F. *Evangelical Theology: A Biblical and Systematic Introduction*. 2nd ed. Grand Rapids: Zondervan, 2020.

Bowens, Lisa M. *African American Readings of Paul: Reception, Resistance, and Transformation*. Grand Rapids: Eerdmans, 2020.

Braxton, Brad Ronnell. *No Longer Slaves: Galatians and African American Experience*. Collegeville, MN: Liturgical, 2002.

Burnside, Jonathan. "Biblical Law and the Scandal of Mass Imprisonment." Paper presented at "The Biblical Mind" conference at the Center for Hebraic Thought, July 20, 2021. https://hebraicthought.org/biblical-law-scandal-mass-imprisonment/.

Campbell, Constantine R. *Basics of Verbal Aspect in Biblical Greek*. Grand Rapids: Zondervan Academic, 2008.

Campbell, Douglas A. "Mass Incarceration: Pauline Problems and Pauline Solutions." *Interpretation* 72 (2018) 251–365.

Cervin, Richard. "Does *kephalē* Mean 'Source' or 'Authority Over' in Greek Literature? A Rebuttal." *Trinity Journal* 10 (1989) 85–112.

Cohick, Lynn H. "Citizenship and Empire: Paul's Letter to the Philippians and Eric Liddell's Work in China." *Journal for the Study of Paul and His Letters* 1 (2011) 14–16.

———. *Ephesians.* NICNT. Grand Rapids: Eerdmans, 2020.

———. "Women, Children, and Families in the Greco-Roman World." In *The World of the New Testament: Cultural, Social, and Historical Contexts*, edited by Joel B. Green and Lee Martin McDonald, 179–88. Grand Rapids: Baker Academic, 2013.

———. *Women in the World of the Earliest Christians: Illuminating Ancient Ways of Life.* Grand Rapids: Baker Academic, 2009.

Demuth, Mary. "I'm Sick of Hearing About Your Smoking Hot Wife." *Christianity Today*, April 19, 2013. https://www.christianitytoday.com/ct/2013/april-web-only/im-sick-of-hearing-about-your-smoking-hot-wife.html.

Dostoevsky, Fyodor. *The Brothers Karamazov.* 1880. https://www.ccel.org/d/dostoevsky/karamozov/htm/book02/chapter04.html.

Emery, Gilles. *The Trinitarian Theology of St. Thomas Aquinas.* Translated by Francesca Aran Murphy. Oxford: Oxford University Press, 2007.

Fee, Gordon D. *The First Epistle to the Corinthians.* NICNT. Grand Rapids: Eerdmans, 1987.

Foster, Paul. "Πίστις Χριστοῦ Terminology in Philippians and Ephesians." In *The Faith of Jesus Christ*, edited by Michael F. Bird and Preston M. Sprinkle, 99–109. Peabody, MA: Hendrickson, 2009.

Gilliard, Dominique Duboi. *Rethinking Incarceration: Advocating for Justice That Restores.* Downers Grove, IL: IVP, 2018.

Gorman, Michael J. *Cruciformity: Paul's Narrative Spirituality of the Cross.* Grand Rapids: Eerdmans, 2001.

———. *Inhabiting the Cruciform God: Kenosis, Justification, and Theosis in Paul's Narrative Soteriology.* Grand Rapids: Eerdmans, 2009.

Green, Joel B. *Conversion in Luke–Acts: Divine Action, Human Cognition, and the People of God.* Grand Rapids: Baker Academic, 2015.

Gregoire, Sheila Wray, et al. *The Great Sex Rescue: The Lies You've Been Taught and How to Recover What God Intended.* Grand Rapids: Baker, 2021.

Grudem, Wayne. "Does *kephalē* ('Head') Mean 'Source' or 'Authority Over' in Greek Literature? A Survey of 2,336 Examples." *Trinity Journal* 6 (1985) 38–59.

———. "The Meaning of *kephalē* ('Head'): An Evaluation of New Evidence, Real and Alleged." *Journal of the Evangelical Theological Society* 44 (2001) 25–65.

Gundry-Volf, Judith M. "The Least and the Greatest: Children in the New Testament." In *The Child in Christian Thought*, edited by Marcia J. Bunge, 29–60. Grand Rapids: Eerdmans, 2001.

Gupta, Nijay K. *Tell Her Story: How Women Led, Taught, and Ministered in the Early Church.* Downers Grove, IL: IVP Academic, 2023.

Harper, Kyle. *From Shame to Sin: The Christian Transformation of Sexual Morality in Late Antiquity.* Cambridge: Harvard University Press, 2013.

Heine, R. E. *Commentaries of Origen and Jerome on St. Paul's Epistle to the Ephesians.* Oxford Early Christian Studies. Oxford: Oxford University Press, 2002.

Hering, James P. *The Colossian and Ephesian Haustafeln in Theological Contexts: An Analysis of their Origins, Relationships, and Message.* New York: Lang, 2007.

Hill, Wesley. *Paul and the Trinity: Persons, Relations, and the Pauline Letters.* Grand Rapids: Eerdmans, 2015.

Hoehner, Harold W. *Ephesians: An Exegetical Commentary.* Grand Rapids: Baker Academic, 2002.

Hylen, Susan E. *Finding Phoebe: What New Testament Women Were Really Like*. Grand Rapids: Eerdmans, 2023.

———. *Women in the New Testament World*. Oxford: Oxford University Press, 2019.

Ilan, Tal. *Lexicon of Jewish Names in Late Antiquity: Part III, The Western Diaspora 333 BCE–650 CE*. Texts and Studies in Ancient Judaism 126. Tübingen: Mohr Siebeck, 2008.

Laes, Christian. *Children in the Roman Empire: Outsiders Within*. Cambridge: Cambridge University Press, 2011.

———. "Desperately Different? *Delicia* Children in the Roman Household." In *Early Christian Families in Context: An Interdisciplinary Dialogue*, edited by David L. Balch and Carolyn Osiek, 298–324. Grand Rapids: Eerdmans, 2003.

———. "Education in Antiquity: Words and Concepts." In *A Cultural History of Education in Antiquity*, 1–10. London: Bloomsbury, 2023.

Langberg, Diane. *Redeeming Power: Understanding Authority and Abuse in the Church*. Grand Rapids: Brazos, 2020.

Lee-Barnewall, Michelle. *Neither Complementarian Nor Egalitarian: Reframing the Gender Debate*. Grand Rapids: Baker Academic, 2016.

———. "Turning ΚΕΦΑΛΗ on Its Head: The Rhetoric of Reversal in Ephesians 5:21–33." In *Christian Origins and Greco-Roman Culture: Social and Literary Contexts for the New Testament*, edited by Stanley E. Porter and Andrew W. Pitts, 605–8. Leiden: Brill, 2013.

Lefkowitz, Mary R., and Maureen B. Fant, eds. *Women's Life in Greece and Rome: A Source Book in Translation*. 4th ed. Baltimore: Johns Hopkins University Press, 2016.

Levine, Amy-Jill. "Bearing False Witness: Common Errors Made About Early Judaism." In *The Jewish Annotated New Testament*, edited by Amy-Jill Levine and Marc Zvi Brettler, 760–63. 2nd ed. Oxford: Oxford University Press, 2011.

———. *Witness at the Cross: A Beginner's Guide to Holy Friday*. Nashville: Abington, 2021.

Leyerle, Blake. "Children and 'the Child' in Early Christianity." In *The Oxford Handbook of Childhood and Education in the Classical World*, edited by Judith Evans Grubbs and Tim Parkin, 559–79. Oxford: Oxford University Press, 2013.

Liddell, Eric H. *The Disciplines of the Christian Life*. New York: Ballantine, 1985.

Lincoln, Andrew T. *Ephesians*. WBC 42. Dallas, TX: Word, 1990.

Lutz, Cora E., trans. *Musonius Rufus: "The Roman Socrates."* Yale Classical Studies 10. New Haven: Yale University Press, 1947.

Lynch, Matt. "Contrary Women: Genesis 3:16b in the (Now Non-)Permanent ESV." https://web.archive.org/web/20161010051528/www.theologicalmisc.net/2016/10/contrary-women-genesis-316b-now-non-permanent-esv/.

MacDonald, Margaret Y. *The Power of Children: The Construction of Families in the Greco-Roman World*. Waco, TX: Baylor University Press, 2014.

Macintosh, A. A. "The Meaning of Hebrew תשוקה." *Journal of Semitic Studies* 61 (2016) 365–87.

Matlock, R. Barry. "Detheologizing the ΠΙΣΤΙΣ ΧΡΙΣΤΟΥ Debate: Cautionary Remarks from a Lexical Semantic Perspective." *Novum Testamentun* 42 (2000) 1–23.

McCaulley, Esau. *Reading While Black: African American Biblical Interpretation as an Exercise in Hope*. Downers Grove, IL: IVP Academic, 2020.

McKnight, Scot. *Pastor Paul: Nurturing a Culture of Christoformity in the Church*. Grand Rapids: Brazos, 2019.

McKnight, Scot, and Laura Barringer. *A Church Called Tov: Forming a Goodness Culture that Resists Abuses of Power and Promotes Healing.* Carol Stream, IL: Tyndale, 2020.

———. *Pivot: The Priorities, Practices, and Powers that Can Transform Your Church into a Tov Culture.* Carol Stream, IL: Tyndale, 2023.

Merkle, Benjamin L. *Ephesians: Exegetical Guide to the Greek New Testament.* Nashville: B&H, 2016.

Mickelsen, Berkeley, and Alvera Mickelsen. "What Does *kephalē* Mean in the New Testament?" In *Women, Authority, and the Bible,* edited by Alvera Mickelsen, 98–99, 105–10. Downers Grove, IL: InterVarsity, 1986.

Mouritsen, Henrik. *The Freedman in the Roman World.* Cambridge: Cambridge University Press, 2011.

Noll, Mark A. *The Civil War as a Theological Crisis.* Chapel Hill, NC: University of North Carolina Press, 2006.

Nussbaum, Martha C. "The Incomplete Feminism of Musonius Rufus, Platonist, Stoic, and Roman." In *The Sleep of Reason: Erotic Experience and Sexual Ethics in Ancient Greece,* edited by Martha C. Nussbaum and Juha Sihvola, 283–325. Chicago: University of Chicago Press, 2002.

Osiek, Carolyn. *Philippians, Philemon.* Abingdon New Testament Commentaries. Nashville: Abingdon, 2000.

Patterson, Orlando. *Slavery and Social Death: A Comparative Study.* Cambridge: Harvard University Press, 1990.

Peeler, Amy. *Women and the Gender of God.* Grand Rapids: Eerdmans, 2022.

Perry, Matthew J. *Gender, Manumission, and the Roman Freedwoman.* Cambridge: Cambridge University Press, 2014.

Peterlin, Davorin. *Paul's Letter to the Philippians in the Light of Disunity in the Church.* Leiden: Brill, 1995.

Rapske, Brian. *The Book of Acts and Paul in Roman Custody.* BAIFCS 3. Grand Rapids: Eerdmans, 1994.

Richards, E. Randolph, and Brandon J. O'Brien. *Misreading Scripture with Western Eyes: Removing Cultural Blinders to Better Understand the Bible.* Downers Grove, IL: InterVarsity, 2012.

Richter, Sandra. "Rape in Israel's World . . . and Ours: A Study of Deuteronomy 22:23–29." *Journal of the Evangelical Theological Society* 64 (2021) 59–76.

Rosner, Brian S. *Greed as Idolatry: The Origin and Meaning of a Pauline Metaphor.* Grand Rapids: Eerdmans, 2007.

Rowlandson, Jane, ed. *Women and Society in Greek and Roman Egypt: A Sourcebook.* Cambridge: Cambridge University Press, 1998.

Ruden, Sarah. *Paul Among the People: The Apostle Reinterpreted and Reimagined in His Own Time.* New York: Image, 2010.

Saller, Richard P. "*Pater Familias, Mater Familias,* and the Gendered Semantics of the Roman Household." *Classical Philology* 94 (1999) 182–97.

Sanders, E. P. *Judaism: Practice and Belief, 63 BCE–66 CE.* Minneapolis: Fortress, 1992.

———. *Paul and Palestinian Judaism: A Comparison of Patterns of Religion.* 40th anniversary ed. Minneapolis: Fortress, 2017.

Shelton, Jo-Ann, and Pauline Ripat, eds. *As the Romans Did: A Source Book in Roman Social History.* 3rd ed. Oxford: Oxford University Press, 2022.

Sigismund-Nielsen, Hanne. "Vibia Perpetua—An Indecent Woman." In *Perpetua's Passions: Multidisciplinary Approaches to the Passio Perpetuae et Felicitatis,* edited by